Police Practice in the '90s

Key Management Issues

Edited by
James J. Fyfe

ICMA

PRACTICAL MANAGEMENT SERIES
Barbara H. Moore, Editor

Police Practice in the '90s
Capital Financing Strategies for Local Governments
Creative Personnel Practices
Current Issues in Leisure Services
The Entrepreneur in Local Government
Ethical Insight, Ethical Action
Hazardous Materials, Hazardous Waste
Human Services on a Limited Budget
Long-Term Financial Planning
Managing New Technologies
Pay and Benefits
Performance Evaluation
Personnel Practices for the '90s
Police Management Today
Practical Financial Management
Risk Management Today
Shaping the Local Economy
Successful Negotiating in Local Government
Telecommunications for Local Government

The Practical Management Series is devoted to the
presentation of information and ideas from diverse
sources. The views expressed in this book are those of
the contributors and are not necessarily those of the
International City Management Association.

Library of Congress Cataloging-in-Publication Data

Police Practice in the '90s: key management issues /
edited by James J. Fyfe.
    p.   cm. -- (Practical management series)
    Includes bibliographical references.
    ISBN 0-87326-058-9
    1. Law enforcement--United States. 2. Police
administration--United States. I. Fyfe, James J.
II. Series.
HV8141.P59 1989
350.74'0973--dc20   89-24451
                                                    CIP

Printed in the United States of America.
949392919089
54321

Police Practice in the '90s: Key Management Issues

The International City Management Association is the professional and educational organization for chief appointed management executives in local government. The purposes of ICMA are to enhance the quality of local government and to nurture and assist professional local government administrators in the United States and other countries. In furtherance of its mission, ICMA develops and disseminates new approaches to management through training programs, information services, and publications.

Managers, carrying a wide range of titles, serve cities, towns, counties, councils of governments, and state/provincial associations of local governments in all parts of the United States and Canada. These managers serve at the direction of elected councils and governing boards. ICMA serves these managers and local governments through many programs that aim at improving the manager's professional competence and strengthening the quality of all local governments.

The International City Management Association was founded in 1914; adopted its City Management Code of Ethics in 1924; and established its Institute for Training in Municipal Administration in 1934. The Institute, in turn, provided the basis for the Municipal Management Series, generally termed the "ICMA Green Books."

ICMA's interests and activities include public management education; standards of ethics for members; the *Municipal Year Book* and other data services; urban research; and newsletters, a monthly magazine, *Public Management*, and other publications. ICMA's efforts for the improvement of local government management—as represented by this book—are offered for all local governments and educational institutions.

About the Editor and Authors

James J. Fyfe is a professor at The American University, School of Public Affairs, Department of Justice, Law and Society, Washington, D.C. He was a New York City police officer for sixteen years and left that agency with the rank of lieutenant. He holds a B.S. degree from the John Jay College of Criminal Justice, City University of New York, and earned his M.A. and Ph.D. degrees from the School of Criminal Justice, State University of New York at Albany. Fyfe is the editor of *Justice Quarterly* and serves on the Commission on Accreditation for Law Enforcement Agencies, Inc.

Following are the affiliations of the contributors to *Police Practice in the '90s: Key Management Issues* at the time of writing:

Cornelius J. Behan, Chief of Police, Baltimore County Police Department, Towson, Maryland, and President, Police Executive Research Forum, Washington, D.C.

Margo Bennett, Special Agent Supervisor, FBI Academy, Quantico, Virginia.

Edward F. Connors III, President, Institute for Law and Justice, Inc., Alexandria, Virginia, and Director, Bureau of Justice Assistance Narcotics Control Technical Assistance Program.

Peter Dodenhoff, Editor, *Law Enforcement News*, John Jay College of Criminal Justice, City University of New York.

John E. Eck, Senior Research Associate and Project Director, Police Executive Research Forum, Washington, D.C.

Sean Grennan, Assistant Professor, Department of Criminal Justice and Security Administration, C. W. Post College, Long Island University, Greenvale, New York.

Vincent Henry, Police Officer, New York City Police Department, and Fulbright Scholar, 1989-1990.

George L. Kelling, Professor of Criminal Justice, Northeastern University, Boston, Massachusetts, and Criminal Justice Policy and Research Fellow, John F. Kennedy School of Government, Harvard University, Cambridge, Massachusetts.

Mark Kroeker, Deputy Chief and Commanding Officer, Personnel and Training Bureau, Los Angeles Police Department, Los Angeles, California.

Barbara Manili, Senior Associate, Institute for Law and Justice, Inc., Alexandria, Virginia.

Stephen D. Mastrofski, Associate Professor, Department of Administration of Justice, The Pennsylvania State University, State College, Pennsylvania.

Candace S. McCoy, Senior Research Associate, United States Sentencing Commission, Washington, D.C.

Phyllis P. McDonald, Director, National Institute of Justice Professional Conference Series, URSA Institute, Bethesda, Maryland.

J. Thomas McEwen, Principal Associate, Institute for Law and Justice, Inc., Alexandria, Virginia.

Mark H. Moore, Daniel and Florence Guggenheim Professor of Criminal Justice Policy and Management, and Faculty Chair, Program in Criminal Justice Policy and Management, John F. Kennedy School of Government, Harvard University, Cambridge, Massachusetts.

Hugh Nugent, Attorney and Principal Associate, Institute for Law and Justice, Inc., Alexandria, Virginia.

Mark Pogrebin, Director, Graduate Program in Criminal Justice, and Co-Director, Law Enforcement Executive Program, Graduate School of Public Affairs, University of Colorado-Denver.

William Spelman, Assistant Professor, Lyndon B. Johnson School of Public Affairs, University of Texas at Austin.

Robert C. Trojanowicz, Director and Professor, School of Criminal Justice, Michigan State University, East Lansing, Michigan, and Criminal Justice Policy and Research Fellow, John F. Kennedy School of Government, Harvard University, Cambridge, Massachusetts.

Edward J. Tully, Chief, Education and Communication Arts, and Director, National Executive Institute, FBI Academy, Quantico, Virginia.

Donald C. Witham, Special Agent, Federal Bureau of Investigation, and Staff Director, Law Enforcement Committee, White House Committee for a Drug Free America, Washington, D.C.

Foreword

One of the most popular books in ICMA's Practical Management Series has been *Police Management Today*, edited by James J. Fyfe and published in 1985. That volume presents in a nutshell the issues that police administrators and local government managers need to consider in making sound decisions about police services in their communities.

Police Practice in the '90s: Key Management Issues builds on the success of that earlier book, reflecting the new challenges that police departments have faced in the years since. The most visible— and possibly the greatest—challenge for the police today is the enormous and frightening incidence of drug-related crime. Faced with this and other problems, the police have embarked on new approaches to their mission—the most popular being community-based or "problem-oriented" policing, in which the police focus their efforts on eradicating problems in the community rather than on reacting to the symptoms of those problems. At the same time, the police field has been moving toward the adoption of standards through departmental accreditation, policy formulation, and professional development.

This new book examines the management issues that accompany these changes. It examines the nature of police leadership today, presents two strong and opposing viewpoints on legalization of drugs, examines policymaking and accreditation, and presents perspectives on personnel and training issues—including supervisory training, burnout among veteran officers, and drug testing of departmental employees.

Like the other books in ICMA's Practical Management Series, this book is devoted to serving the needs of local government managers, department administrators, and students for timely information on current issues and problems.

We are grateful to James J. Fyfe, who organized and compiled the volume, to the individuals who contributed articles, and to the organizations that granted ICMA permission to reprint their materials.

William H. Hansell
Executive Director
International City
Management Association

Contents

Introduction

James J. Fyfe

This is the second time in five years that I have had the privilege of editing a volume in ICMA's Practical Management Series. Much has happened since then and, hopefully, this book has kept apace of the major concerns of practitioners, students, and other observers of local government and policing.

One constant over the last five years, and, indeed, over the history of organizations, is that no single individual is more critical to success or failure than the person at the top. Another is that even strong and talented leaders cannot guarantee success or maximum effectiveness if they occupy the top boxes of inappropriately arranged organizational charts. Thus, Part 1 of this book is given over to questions of police leadership and organization.

First, Donald C. Witham brings readers up-to-date on the state of police leadership in America. Witham's article summarizes the results of his Police Executive Research Forum (PERF) survey of police chief executives in departments employing 75 or more personnel.[1] The results may surprise readers who have grown accustomed to reading that police chiefs hang on to their jobs about as long as beauty contest winners hold their crowns, or that chiefs are parochial, undereducated, and underqualified political hacks. The chiefs Witham studied averaged 5.5 years in their current position. More than half had worked in at least one other police agency, and one in ten had been chief of another agency. Better than half held baccalaureate degrees, and about a quarter held graduate degrees. In short, Witham's respondents gave him good cause to be optimistic about the current state of American police leadership and its future.

That's the good news. Less likely to warm the hearts of readers is Stephen D. Mastrofski's message that one anticipated panacea for some of the problems facing police—consolidation of the services of small agencies—may not be all it was cracked up to be. Mastrofski worked with a council of governments in rural Pennsylvania where decisionmakers were eager to explore the feasibility and desirability of consolidating police service delivery. After striking organizational, logistical, economic, and political rocks, however, this exploration ended where it started, and no consolidation was accomplished. The trip was not a total loss, because much was learned *en route*. Perhaps the most important lesson was that there are many valid impediments to consolidation. Mastrofski concludes that neither the people with whom he worked nor interested readers need to regard the failure to consolidate as "a victory for irrational 'political considerations.'" It simply may be the best choice in a particular situation.

The next group of selections discuss the police mission. The first article was written by Mark H. Moore, Robert C. Trojanowicz, and George L. Kelling, three of the most renowned police scholars in the country. They begin their article unequivocally: "The core mission of the police is to control crime. No one disputes this."

Because many others have convincingly defined the core mission of the police in terms other than crime control, readers may not be as confident as these three authors that their first statement is correct.[2] Further, because of the mere existence of these alternate definitions of the police mission, their second assertion must be incorrect. Those who know these authors, however, will be aware that they opened their article in this manner specifically to be provocative.

The article, written with National Institute of Justice funding for the Harvard Program in Criminal Justice Policy and Management, surveys the research on street crime and police crime control strategies and their effectiveness. The authors point out that police strategies have historically had little demonstrable effect on crime or public safety. They argue, however, that the early evidence suggests that emerging "problem-solving" and "community-oriented" styles of policing are effective in achieving what they define as the core mission of the police. This article should be especially illuminating to city managers and other officials whose work does not involve daily exposure to the literature and research on police crimefighting strategies and trends.

This article also leads logically to William Spelman and John E. Eck's explication of new problem-oriented policing models. Spelman and Eck, who have been active since the beginning of this movement, offer readers concepts and examples to show that problem-oriented policing is considerably more than the latest fad, and that its successes have been demonstrable. This alternate model of policing defines and systematizes what innovative beat cops in tradition-bound agencies have done on their own for decades. Equally important, to paraphrase Spelman and Eck, it raises to the level of official policy these officers' interest in doing things right rather than in doing what rigid bureaucratic models prescribe as the right thing.

At the same time, some observers believe that the initial enthusiasm for problem-oriented policing needs to be tempered by past experience with promising new ideas that, over the long haul, have failed to meet expectations. Mastrofski writes of one; Moore, Trojanowicz, and Kelling write of several. While this new model has much to offer, time will be the only true test of its effectiveness.

Perhaps the most time-consuming, costly, and controversial issue facing the police today is drug enforcement. The issue, which raises substantial philosophical and operational questions, has given rise to a major debate on the wisdom, efficacy, and practicality of legalizing drugs. This book presents two opposing views from this debate.

On one side is Arnold S. Trebach, one of the most provocative figures in the criminal justice community. Trebach has been at the center of the current debate on drug policy since he published the first of his two books on the subject in 1982,[3] and many in policing and government view him as an extremist. In reading his interview with Peter Dodenhoff, the reader may note that there is an allegory between Trebach's work on drug policy and the work of more "mainstream" police researchers whose writings are included in this volume. In their article, Moore, Trojanowicz, and Kelling point out that the historical strategies of the police war on crime have accomplished little. They suggest an alternative model, and Spelman and Eck give substance to their suggestion. Trebach says precisely the same thing about drug abuse, which, he is the first to acknowledge, is at the head of the list of America's social problems. In Trebach's view, both social science data and a walk on inner-city streets demonstrate that the war on drugs has not worked. Thus, he concludes, it is time to begin redefining the drug problem and to explore new ways of dealing with it. As readers will discover, August Vollmer, the pioneer of American police professionalism, held almost precisely the same views in 1936.

Other responsible people, of course, have reached contrary conclusions after examining precisely the same data and walking the same inner-city streets. One influential group with an opposing view is the Major City Chiefs of Police, a group of forty-eight among the FBI Academy's National Executive Institute Associates. Edward J. Tully and Margo Bennett synthesize the chiefs' views on strategies for dealing with the drug problem. Not surprisingly, these chiefs do not agree with Trebach on strategy or on the definition of success in dealing with the drug problem. Both sides of the argument, however, have in common good faith and a deep concern for the impact of drugs on our society and its health, and both sides are eager to minimize it.

One of the most promising trends in American policing is the movement toward articulation of professional standards and criteria for police decision making. Thus, the four articles in Part 3 deal with professional police standards and policies.

This, again, is a sensitive area. Many in policing have historically opposed the formulation of guidelines and standards on the grounds that they unrealistically restrict police flexibility and discretion and that they impose Big Brother style uniformity on a function that must be responsive to local differences. This view is rapidly disappearing as policing moves in the direction of increasing professionalization.

The fact is that police have historically held virtually unlimited discretion and that we are centuries from anything resembling Big Brother. In many jurisdictions, the most critical police decisions— when to use force, when to shoot, when to pursue a vehicle, when to attempt to run a vehicle off the road—have been limited only by criminal law. The criminal law, most police have come to realize, is simply too broad to serve as the criterion for the exercise of professional discretion, and must be supplemented by standards that reflect the best professional thinking. At the same time, where policing is concerned, these standards cannot be so rigid that they weaken local authority over police.

Some of the best professional thinking on police standards has come from the International Association of Chiefs of Police (IACP) National Law Enforcement Policy Center, which has asked some of IACP's most knowledgeable members to identify critical policy areas and to develop model policy statements for them. Phyllis P. McDonald, former director of the center, has contributed an article on the value of policy formulation and the techniques used in creating a departmental policy manual.

Mark Kroeker and Candace S. McCoy address the policy issue from a different perspective. They emphasize the value of policies to street-level police officers and point out that, since these officers must implement such policies, they must have some input into them and must be thoroughly trained in them. In policing, Kroeker and McCoy suggest, no plan from the top can be successfully implemented unless those at the bottom understand it and buy into its logic and goals. Too often, this valuable advice has been overlooked by well-meaning administrators who come to find that their best-laid plans fail because they have not taken adequate measures to implement them.

My own chapter on police vehicle pursuits is designed to aid in formulation of policy in this critical area. Pursuits are a very emotional issue for police, because each potential pursuit situation forces officers to weigh their obligation to protect life against their desire and duty to apprehend offenders. I have attempted to evaluate these concerns, to summarize the most recent data, and to make concrete policy recommendations.

A major influence on the adoption of standards by police departments has been the Commission on Accreditation for Law Enforcement Agencies, Inc. (CALEA). One of the early champions of accreditation, and one of the first chiefs to see his department through the process, was Cornelius J. Behan of Baltimore County, Maryland. His article, which explains the accreditation process and points out its benefits, represents the view of those who argue that accreditation is a prerequisite to professional status for police.

As a commissioner of CALEA, I have heard many objections to accreditation as well. If this is such a good thing, I am asked, why do police departments have to pay to become accredited? My department is doing a good job now; why should I have to go through the agony of conforming to hundreds of standards made up by people I don't know?

So far, I have not found it difficult to answer these questions. Police departments that apply must foot a bill for accreditation for the same reason that universities and hospitals do. Accreditation is certification that an institution conforms to the standards of a profession. The profession finds the funds to develop its standards, but it is the responsibility of the individual institutions within the profession to pay for the process of determining whether they conform.

The second major question about accreditation—who are those guys?—also has a relatively simple answer that is consistent with Kroeker and McCoy's thesis that those who implement police policy must have input into police policy. CALEA's standards were developed by representatives of IACP, PERF, the National Organization of Black Law Enforcement Executives, and the National Sheriffs' Association. The members of these organizations are the people who manage American police departments and who knew that they would have to implement the standards that their representatives devised. They then made sure that the standards were sound, yet general and flexible enough to be tailored to any law enforcement agency's needs. Even for law enforcement agencies that choose not to go through the admittedly agonizing accreditation process, CALEA's standards provide a guide to what the major professional organizations view as the state of the police art. They should be on the bookshelf of every municipal official.

Part 4 begins with an article written by Vincent Henry and Sean Grennan, who describe police supervisory and middle management training in the nation's three largest police departments. Their analyses show that the topics covered in training programs for new sergeants and lieutenants differ significantly among these three departments. The differences lead Henry and Grennan to the view that there is no single right answer to the question of what police supervisors need to know. They do conclude, however, that some degree of formal training is necessary for anybody taking a step up the ranks of a police agency.

The burned-out cop is a staple of second-rate paperbacks, movies, and television shows. Unfortunately, the burned-out cop exists in virtually every police department. He—or more recently, she—has typically advanced no further than the entry level, feels abused and unrecognized, and may express hostility and frustration in very destructive ways. In "Alienation among Veteran Police Officers," Mark Pogrebin describes his studies of burned-out cops and offers suggestions as to how their alienation and frustration may be prevented and minimized. One of the themes underlying Pogrebin's work, like that of other writers, is that the burned-out cop is usually a product of management insensitivity. Consequently, if Pogrebin is correct, much burnout among field officers can be prevented by greater management sensitivity.

The last selection touches an ugly subject: drug abuse among police personnel. Originally commissioned by the National Institute of Justice and published in 1986, it has been updated for this volume by Hugh Nugent, who collaborated on the original piece with coauthors Edward F. Connors III, J. Thomas McEwen, and Barbara Manili. This is a critical piece, because it defines police authority to determine whether officers engage in criminal activity of a sort that strikes at the core of police integrity.

I began this introduction by noting that changes have occurred in the police field over the last five years. Most of these changes have been net gains.

Two exceptions are the irreplaceable losses of people who contributed to my first book in the Practical Management Series and who, more importantly, made major impacts on policing and public administration.

Gary P. Hayes, the first executive director of the Police Executive Research Forum, helped to conceptualize the first book, *Police Management Today*, and was a sounding board for my ideas during the years in which I was privileged to know him. The work of Charles H. Levine was first brought to my attention by Barbara Moore, editor of the Practical Management Series. I included Levine's work on strategic management in the 1985 book, and did not come to know him until later, when he was appointed Distinguished Professor of Public Administration at my university.

The business of running government and the police will not be the same without Gary and Charley, and this book is dedicated to them.

1. For a full presentation see: Donald C. Witham, *The American Law Enforcement Chief Executive: A Management Profile* (Washington, DC: Police Executive Research Forum, 1985).

2. See, especially: Egon Bittner, *The Functions of the Police in Modern Society* (Rockville, MD: National Institute of Mental Health, 1970) and James Q. Wilson, *Varieties of Police Behavior* (Cambridge, MA: Harvard University Press, 1968). Bittner argues that the core of the police mission is to hold an official monopoly on the use of coercive force; Wilson states that the police mission is to maintain order, a task that, in practice, sometimes requires that the police overlook minor crimes.

3. Arnold S. Trebach, *The Heroin Solution* (New Haven, CT: Yale University Press, 1982) and *The Great Drug War* (New York: McMillan, 1987).

PART 1

Police Leadership
and Organization

Transformational Police Leadership

—————————————————————————— Donald C. Witham

During the past decade, two seminal works on leadership have been published. In 1978, James McGregor Burns wrote a Pulitzer Prize winning book entitled *Leadership*.[1] Burns wrote that leadership is one of the most observed, but least understood, phenomena in the world. In 1985, Warren Bennis and Burt Nanus authored another important book, *Leaders: Strategies for Taking Charge*.[2] Bennis and Nanus built upon Burns' idea of a transformational leader, and they describe the essential roles that leaders and executives play with respect to organizational success and performance. According to these authors, the distinguishing talent possessed by transformational leaders is the ability to envision. They are capable of seeing the entire organization, the complex environment, and the interaction of the two as a single entity. Further, they are able to project this view into the future and describe a favorable future for the organization. They articulate this vision to others and provide them with a sense of meaning. Also, they inspire trust in others—partly because of their steadfastness to their vision.[3] These works have significantly advanced our understanding of the subject of leadership and brought tangible insights and guidance to students and practitioners of leadership.

This article will examine the background and preparation of police leaders in America, and it will speculate as to how these experiences may relate to their ability to envision. In particular, four areas of their preparation will be highlighted—range of police and managerial experience, level of formal education, extent of professional development or training, and involvement with community

Reprinted from the *FBI Law Enforcement Bulletin*, December 1987.

and other groups outside law enforcement. The author believes these factors are important developmental elements for successful police leadership.

Law enforcement executives

The literature on law enforcement has long been critical of the inadequacies of police executives as they attempt to discharge their responsibilities. Raymond Fosdick's classic book, *American Police Systems*, was published in 1920, and even then he criticized the performance of police executives:

> Far more than to any other factor, the irrational development of American police organization is due to inadequate leadership. To the lack of trained and intelligent administrators, obtaining and holding office on favorable conditions, much of the confusion and maladjustment of our police machinery is ascribable.[4]

Upgrading the quality of American law enforcement has been an important national goal over the last two decades. A number of task forces and commissions have developed a host of recommendations. Interestingly, few of these recommendations relate directly to police leaders. The bulk of the suggestions pertain to setting standards for police recruits in areas such as training and education. Such a bottom-up approach will eventually result in improvements in law enforcement.

Perhaps, however, a more immediate approach to upgrading law enforcement would focus upon police leaders and executives. Although no single group can bring about enhanced law enforcement competence, no other group is better positioned to effect this transformation than police administrators.

Virtually every study or commission to examine American law enforcement since Fosdick's time also has been quite critical of law enforcement administrators. Despite an awareness of the complexity of the law enforcement executive's position and an awareness of the historical inadequacies of law enforcement leadership, and furthermore, despite substantial efforts in the last decades to upgrade American law enforcement, there has been practically no comprehensive research on this subject. This article will describe some selected findings of a study of law enforcement executives contained in *The American Law Enforcement Chief Executive: A Management Profile* published by the Police Executive Research Forum (PERF) in 1985.[5]

The PERF study

During 1982 and late 1983, nearly 500 police chief executives from throughout the United States participated in a major PERF study. The executives headed the larger state, county, or municipal departments in the nation (i.e., a minimum of 75 full-time employees). Every state in the nation was represented by at least one executive, with the exception of Vermont. The extremely high response rates achieved by the two surveys (88% and 90% respectively) added greatly to the quality of this research. At the same time, the response rates indicate the high level of conscientiousness of the administrators and their dedication to quality policing in America. Chart 1 contains some profile data on police executives.

Chart 1. Profile of police executive

A. The chief executive

1. Age .... 49 years
2. Time in present position .... 5.5 years
3. Law enforcement experience .... 24 years
4. Experience in present department .... 17.7 years
5. Work week .... 56.6 hours
6. Experience in law enforcement before becoming
   executive 92%
7. Promoted to chief's position from another
   executive position within law enforcement 80%
8. Previous experience as a chief executive in
   another law enforcement agency 10.5%
9. Experience in at least one other law
   enforcement agency 54.9%

B. Education level
1. Minimum of a baccalaureate degree 50.7% (1982)
                                                         56.8% (1983)
2. Graduate degree 18.4% (1982)
                                                         25.6% (1983)
3. Associate degree 17.1% (1982)
                                                         15.9% (1983)
4. Less than an associate degree 32.2% (1982)
                                                         27.3% (1983)
5. Most common field of study (minimum of an
   associate degree)
   a. Law enforcement—criminal justice 49.5%
   b. Public—business administration 29%

C. Executive development training needs (highest
   rated subject areas 1982 and 1983)
1. Executive's role in management
2. Legal problems and issues
3. Personnel management
4. Strategic planning
5. Computers and information management

Discussion of selected findings

This section will describe those findings believed to relate to the executives' ability to become transformational leaders. First, the mean age of the participants was 49. In the chart, items 1–5 under Heading A—"The Chief Executive"—are all statistical means of the data. Readers interested in a more detailed description of the methodology or statistical analysis can find that information in the book, *The American Law Enforcement Chief Executive: A Management Profile*. The respondents were not young, impressionable men, but veterans of nearly 25 years of policing. In fact, since over 90 percent of the respondents had prior police experience and the entire group averaged over 17 years in their present department, it's quite clear that only a few could have had recent experience in other occupations or even other police agencies. Previous research has criticized the relatively narrow experience (e.g., primarily within one police agency for many years) of law enforcement administrators. This condition appears to remain largely unchanged, and such a narrow range of experience would not seem conducive to developing a sophisticated understanding of the complex environment in which policing must function.

The educational levels achieved by the participants far exceed the levels discovered during previous research. There can be no question that law enforcement leaders have made substantial progress in this area. Again, this is an area in which the field has been harshly criticized in earlier studies. As recently as 1975, an International Association of Chiefs of Police (IACP) study found that only about 10 percent of chiefs nationwide had earned a baccalaureate degree.[6]

The percentages of college graduates among the chiefs differed markedly by region. Executives from the western region were twice as likely to have a degree as their colleagues from the northeast. Executives in the south and north central fell between the two extremes, but their percentages were much closer to their western colleagues than to their northeastern counterparts.

There was a strong consensus among the respondents that executive development training programs were excellent vehicles for improving the performance of administrators. In fact, the executives overwhelmingly selected training over other methods (e.g., more experience or education) to prepare their successors properly for the top position. Also, some respondents wrote that law enforcement has a distance yet to travel in executive training before it catches up with other types of training in the field.

The final selected finding related to how the administrators viewed their jobs. They were requested to rate their three most important duties from a list of nine functions that are frequently described within the management literature as executive in nature (e.g., identify and set objectives or establish priorities). It was obvious from their ratings that many of the chiefs realize that there is more to their job than administering a complex police organization. A number of executives rated maintaining relationships with community leaders, political figures, and the media as integral to their effectiveness. These officials know that law enforcement is a public function that will never be truly apolitical, and that if they are going to be effective in their role, they must interact with a number of significant actors outside of their organizations. This vision, which comprehends the political environment in which law enforcement occurs, was not as broadly shared as might be expected.

Preparing for transformational leadership

The thumbnail sketch in the first section of this article includes the essential elements of transformational leadership. Still, readers are strongly encouraged to read the Bennis and Nanus book in its entirety to receive a thorough explanation of their ideas. To avoid misunderstanding here, two critical points will be discussed more completely. First, the ability to articulate a vision of where an organization is going is not synonymous with being glib or quick witted. It is much more. Most especially, it entails sound and careful thinking. Further, steadfastness to the vision described implies more than bullheadedness. In particular, it means that people trust a leader's integrity and character. Thus, transformational leadership addresses and stresses the morality and integrity of leaders unlike some of the fashionable but simplistic approaches so popular in recent years.

How does one go about developing the ability to envision? Or, how does one learn to make a mesh of things? Clearly, there are no guaranteed approaches or methods; however, it seems quite sensible to argue that by putting people in a wide variety of jobs and situations, and requiring them to think seriously about their lives, their profession, and their nation, perhaps the broadening process can be facilitated. Some people will never see the big picture regardless of their preparation. Still, the four aspects of preparation discussed here can assist many individuals in furthering their understanding of law enforcement in America.

If there is any truth to the old saying that what you see depends on where you sit, then aspiring executives should attempt to sit in as many different chairs as possible. In this way, they can begin to see situations from a variety of viewpoints or perspectives.

At present, it seems unrealistic to expect many police leaders to serve in more than one department so they can gain these varied perspectives. In general, pension systems do not allow for this sort of mobility without imposing some level of risk to the financial security of the executive and his family. Nevertheless, future police leaders should give careful consideration to their career plans to allow for as many different types of jobs and experiences as possible. Several participants in the PERF study indicated that administrative positions were particularly beneficial experiences for understanding the chief's position, and that in some departments, these positions were not as career enhancing as operational-type positions. Aspiring chiefs should attempt to complete both types of assignments.

The reasons for advocating that law enforcement officials have regular involvement with community and professional figures are essentially the same as those just described regarding career planning. This contact will insure that officials expose themselves to a wide variety of opinions and views. Many innovative ideas from one occupation can be adapted by other fields, and leaders must constantly scan their communities and professional discipline for new ideas. Probably an even more compelling reason for this involvement is that police organizations exist to serve the citizenry. Is there a better method to receive feedback on organizational performance than directly from influential community figures?

With respect to the necessity for a formal education, including at least a baccalaureate degree, and the need for quality developmental and executive training programs, this sort of preparation insures that administrators have been exposed to current concepts and opinions on numerous matters relevant to law enforcement. These intellectually stimulating experiences can assist executives in developing an open and inquiring mind. They should help leaders obtain a more refined understanding of the proper role of law enforcement in American society. This understanding is crucial to forming a vision of the future of the organization. Even though this knowledge is somewhat intangible and may be difficult to discern, it informs most of the daily actions and decisions of the administrators. Author Harlan Cleveland believes that there is a bright future for complexity.[7] If this is so, can anyone doubt the importance of sound intellectual preparation for police leaders?

Conclusion

It is widely recognized that the most critical ingredient in the success of an organization is the quality of its leadership.[8] Although police leaders cannot singlehandedly upgrade law enforcement, there is no other single group as important to this process. Further, police organizations, like their counterparts elsewhere, need transformational leaders to successfully confront the challenges of the future. The author believes that certain types of preparation and experience can assist an individual in developing this critical skill.

Finally, increasing fiscal pressures on all governments cannot be allowed to impede the continued upgrading of American law enforcement. Law enforcement is too important a governmental function, and good policing too important a right of all citizens and legal residents, to be sacrificed on the altar of cutback management. The real progress in policing of the last 20 years can not be allowed to dissipate. Individuals of the highest moral character and with solid intellectual ability are required to lead law enforcement agencies. Now is the time to take stock and move forward.

1. James McGregor Burns, *Leadership* (New York: Harper & Row, 1978).
2. Warren Bennis and Burt Nanus, *Leaders: Strategies for Taking Charge* (New York: Harper & Row, 1985).
3. Ibid., pp. 216–219.
4. Raymond Fosdick, *American Police Systems*, reprinted (Montclair, NJ: Patterson Smith, 1969), p. 215.
5. Donald C. Witham, *The American Law Enforcement Chief Executive: A Management Profile* (Washington, DC: Police Executive Research Forum, 1985).
6. National Advisory Commission on Criminal Justice Standards and Goals, *Police Chief Executive*, PCE Report (Washington, DC: Government Printing Office, 1976), Appendix D.
7. Harlan Cleveland, *The Future Executive: A Guide for Tomorrow's Managers* (New York: Harper & Row, 1972), p. 7.
8. Bennis and Nanus, *Leaders*, pp. 226–27.

Police Agency Consolidation: Lessons from a Case Study

Stephen D. Mastrofski

In the decade following the publication of *The Challenge of Crime in a Free Society* in 1967,[1] police agency consolidation was an important item on the agenda of police reform in America. A number of highly visible blue-ribbon commissions called for consolidating small police agencies, reasoning that consolidation would foster interdepartmental coordination and prevent wasteful duplication of services while increasing both the quantity and the professional quality of service.[2] But by 1980 a scholar who had carefully traced the history of the consolidation movement declared the movement a failure, a victim of the enduring appeal of the "American tradition of localism in the delivery of police service."[3]

Even if agency consolidation is no longer a major focus of police reform efforts at the national level, it remains an issue for many communities. A nationwide survey of 2,089 cities and counties of all sizes found that 203 interjurisdictional transfers of public safety or correctional services had occurred between 1976 and 1983.[4] In the area of police and fire communications alone, 2.5 percent of the responding jurisdictions reported intergovernmental transfers of responsibility for service. In addition, in 1983, 49.7 percent of the responding jurisdictions reported entering into intergovernmental service contracts for public safety and correctional services. Of course, these figures do not include jurisdictions that had considered some form of police consolidation but decided against it.

Local advocates of consolidation frequently equate growth in agency size with improvements in performance. They express frustration at the failure of their communities to appreciate the benefits of service from a larger police organization. Local opponents of consolidation claim that consolidating police services detracts from the special identity of each community and deprives its residents of the capacity to shape police services to suit that identity. This difference of opinion often boils down to an all-or-nothing debate between two opposing extreme views: that "bigger is better" and that "small is beautiful."

Neither position is of much value to communities considering whether to consolidate police services. There is so much variability among American communities that it is risky to make broad generalizations.

Police consolidation is an issue for decisionmakers to address rationally, and they must analyze the local situation with care before venturing a prediction about its consequences. Deciding whether to consolidate usually means weighing a number of competing priorities on the basis of only scant data regarding the consequences of these alternatives. This article shows how local jurisdictions can conduct inquiries into the possibility of consolidation to make the most informed decisions about whether and how to consolidate. It uses as an example the author's experience as a consultant to the Centre Region (Pennsylvania) Council of Governments, which wished to explore the feasibility and desirability of consolidating police service delivery for several of its member municipalities.

What is police agency consolidation?

Police agency consolidation is a reduction in the number of police agencies providing service to a given jurisdiction or group of jurisdictions. It can occur in a number of ways. Entire governments can be merged, with police being part of the merger. Alternatively, governments can retain their separate identities but form a federation that uses a common (sometimes called "metropolitan") force created by the merger of two or more police departments. Such mergers often are called "total" consolidations; they have occurred in such places as Nashville-Davidson (Tennessee), Jacksonville-Duval (Florida), Clark–Las Vegas (Nevada), Miami-Dade (Florida), and Metropolitan Toronto (Ontario, Canada). Far more frequent is consolidation accomplished via contract, where a jurisdiction disbands its own force (or never forms one) and contracts with another jurisdiction for the provision of police services. The Los Angeles County Sheriff's Department has this arrangement with thirty cities.[5] Some sheriffs and state police are obliged by law to provide services without fee to incorporated areas that have not formed their own full-time law enforcement organizations. Police services may be provided part-time if the jurisdiction has its own part-time police force. Finally, some consolidations encompass only some police functions. In these functional consolidations, which are common between small municipal departments and county sheriffs or state police, the municipalities provide patrol service, and the county or state agency provides investigative and other specialist services. Sometimes several metropolitan departments contribute personnel and equipment to form specialist squads for major crimes or narcotics. Increasingly, auxiliary services such as communications, detention, evidence analysis, and training are functionally consolidated. A large police agency may provide one or more of these services, sometimes on a contract basis; or a separate organizational entity may be created, such as a regional lab, training facility, or countywide emergency communications center.

Research on consolidation

Research evidence on the consequences of police agency consolidation is neither strong nor unequivocal. Where consolidation has occurred, researchers have been unable to attribute any changes in agency performance to consolidation rather than to other influences. Studies have suggested that consolidation does not often result in economies of scale.[6] Evaluations of consolidation by contract show mixed results: some indicate greater efficiency,[7] while others indicate higher unit costs and no improvement in service quality.[8]

Some researchers have attempted to learn about the effects of consolidation by comparing departments of differing size at the same point in time. The results of these studies have generally been more favorable for small departments than for larger ones. In small departments, wasteful duplication of service is rare and interdepartmental coordination is the norm, suggesting that fragmenting service delivery among many smaller departments in a metropolitan area is not inherently inefficient.[9] Indeed, such fragmented arrangements seem to offer the greatest potential for enhancing agency productivity in terms of the number of cars on the street and clearances by arrest per officer.[10]

A number of detailed studies of small and large departments suggest that when neighborhoods are matched for socioeconomic and demographic features, smaller agencies tend to produce higher levels of satisfaction among their residents than do larger agencies.[11] This pattern is far from uniform, however, and sometimes medium-sized departments (51 to 160 sworn) outperform the smallest and largest agencies in terms of the public's evaluation of their personal experiences and of the department in general. These studies have been criticized on a variety of methodological grounds—for example, the method of selecting departments and neighborhoods for comparison and the emphasis on citizens' subjective assessments as performance criteria.[12] Using different measures and different designs, critics have found only weak relationships between the size of police agencies and quality of performance. One study, based on neither citizen evaluations nor agency performance records, found that size of department was unrelated to many aspects of police behavior that were recorded by ride-along observers: initiating service to citizens, making residential security checks, making suspect stops, rendering comfort and assistance, making arrests, and officer demeanor). However, officers in smaller departments were much less likely to use force in nonthreatening situations and much more likely to show that they were acquainted with members of the public whom they encountered.[13] Unfortunately, the study did not include any department smaller than 53 officers, thus excluding those that are most often the target of proconsolidation forces.

The debate continues over the appropriate research methodology and measures to evaluate structural arrangements for policing. Although much research has cast doubt on the benefits of consolidation, no findings have demonstrated unequivocally that departments should avoid consolidation. Thus, each situation deserves close analysis and a consideration of the widest possible variety of options. This was, in fact, the approach taken by the Centre Region Council of Governments.

The Centre Region experience

In 1984 the Centre Region Council of Governments (COG) contracted with a consultant to study existing arrangements for provision of police services among several of its member governments and to explore the feasibility and merits of alternative arrangements. The COG is a confederation of six municipal governments (five townships and a borough). In Pennsylvania, both boroughs and townships have the status of municipality. Each municipality has the council-manager form of government and has its own staff that provides a number of services to the citizens of the Centre Region: code enforcement, parks and recreation, regional planning, library services, and senior citizen services. As a policy-making body the COG had been a focal point for debate over the merits of various forms of intergovernmental coordination. Increasing cooperation and coordination among local police service providers had been under discussion for several years, and COG members felt that they needed more detailed information to make informed decisions about altering structural arrangements, possibly by some form of consolidation.

The COG members appointed representatives to an advisory task force of police officials and municipal managers that would formulate alternatives for the consultant to assess. The Pennsylvania State Police and the Pennsylvania State University, also providers of local police service, were invited to appoint representatives as well. The task force was charged to develop alternatives for restructuring intergovernmental arrangements for service delivery, ranging from increased coordination to consolidation of selected functions to major realignments in the delivery of primary services (through total consolidation, contracting, and state police involvement). The task force, coordinated by the consultant, was to develop in considerable detail the most administratively feasible plans and to specify how they could be implemented. The task force also was to provide the consultant with data that would help him estimate the cost and organizational implications of each alternative. Neither the task force nor the consultant was to recommend a specific alternative. Rather, their role was to provide information that would allow elected officials to decide how to proceed.

The Centre Region forms the population core of a small metropolitan area in the middle of the state, far removed from other metropolitan areas. It is the home of the Pennsylvania State University, which dominates the local economy and demography. Table 1 lists the residential populations, crime rates, and calls for service of the five municipalities participating in the study (one member jurisdiction of the COG did not participate). The area frequently is mentioned in national surveys as a very desirable area in which to live and was once listed as the "least stressful" area in the United States, in part because of the relatively low level of reported crime.

At the time of the study, five full-time police departments served the participating jurisdictions: the borough of State College Bureau of Police Services (50 sworn, 12 civilian), the Ferguson Township Police (8 sworn, 1 civilian), the Patton Township Police (8 sworn, 1 civilian), the Pennsylvania State University Department of Safety (37 sworn, 8 full-time civilian—not included in the analysis in this article), and a station of the Pennsylvania State Police (40 sworn, 4 civilian). Each municipal department provided services to its own jurisdiction, and in addition, State College provided service on a contract basis to College and Harris townships. The state police committed their routine service delivery to rural areas and small towns, mostly outside the Centre Region, although they supplemented municipal departments on request. The State College police

Table 1. Population, crime, and police service demand in the Centre Region.

| Characteristic | Jurisdiction receiving service | | | | |
	State College	College	Harris	Ferguson	Patton
Population	37,274[a]	6,453[a]	3,185	7,923	7,964
1983 Part I crimes/100 pop.	3.7	[b]	[b]	1.9	1.8
1983 Part II crimes/100 pop.	7.0	[b]	[b]	5.2	3.7
1983 calls for service/100 pop.	31.0	41.0	20.0	26.0	27.0

[a] Excludes on-campus residents.
[b] College and Harris Township crimes are included in State College reports.

provided communications service and a computerized warrant file for all of the municipalities in the study, funded by a contract with Centre County. Officers of the Patton and Ferguson township departments were cross-deputized and frequently provided backup and routine patrol services for each other when training and vacations reduced staffing levels. All of the departments had a long history of close coordination and cooperation in a variety of areas: traffic regulation during major university and regional events, training, criminal investigations, and a youth development camp. Police administrators often met informally, and the relationships among departments were cordial.

Elected officials and public figures throughout the region had repeatedly expressed interest in consolidating local governments or particular services, such as police services. Some felt that a regionwide consolidation was the way to achieve economies of scale, increase professionalism, and deal with regional problems in a more uniform fashion. Troubled by the rising cost and by the terms of contract services, some township spokespersons were interested in exploring arrangements that would keep costs down without decreasing services. Underlying the interest in new alternatives was the townships' desire to maintain their own identity and control of services independent of the much larger State College borough government. In addition, many borough spokespersons had expressed concern that the borough not enter into arrangements that would significantly dilute its capacity to shape police services to the special needs of that community, a more densely populated area with a downtown and a large off-campus student population. Although doubts about specific proposals had been expressed, no active core of advocacy or opposition for a specific line of action had arisen in any of the municipalities. Indeed, public leaders uniformly expressed satisfaction with the quality of police services they were receiving under existing arrangements; their motivation appeared to be to find ways to make arrangements even better, if possible.

The options

During many meetings over several months, the advisory task force developed thirteen specific proposals for altering the arrangements for service delivery. Most involved modest changes in the level of interorganizational cooperation and coordination, but four proposals outlined options that rearranged who provided service to whom and on what basis.

Existing arrangements   The two townships that contracted with the borough of State College received given amounts of service at specified rates: College Township received 195 hours per week and Harris received 90. Costs were adjusted annually, and contracts were automatically renewed annually unless either party gave written notice of termination at least one year in advance. Although decisions about the allocation of resources, tactics, and strategies were routinely left to the borough police chief, township governments could articulate specific concerns and requests through their managers to the borough chief.

The demands placed on the police varied among the five municipalities, although not as much as some might expect. Levels of reported crime per capita in the borough (including College and Harris crimes—see Table 1) were 1.5 to 2 times those in Ferguson and Patton townships, but the number of calls for service per capita did not differ nearly as much. In all jurisdictions the vast majority of service incidents involved traffic, minor offenses and disturbances, and miscellaneous services. There appeared to be no major incompatibilities among the jurisdictions in the range of police services needed.

There were significant differences among the four existing police departments covered in this analysis, but also many similarities. The smaller departments had very little specialization, concentrating mostly on patrol services. The chiefs performed administrative and supervisory duties as well as direct service to the community. The borough and state police departments had considerably greater specialization of functions (e.g., criminal investigations) and a larger proportion of personnel committed to supervisory and administrative functions. The borough and state police agencies also had more extensive formalization of rules, policies, and records than the township departments. The principal operating difference among them, however, was that the state police, as a matter of statewide policy, did not enforce local ordinances, whereas the municipal agencies did. Officers in the borough and the Patton Township departments were represented by bargaining units. Although state police troopers received considerably more basic training than municipal officers, the departments were otherwise roughly comparable in the educational background and amount of training received by their officers—with the exception of Patton Township, which provided significantly lower levels of annual training. The borough and the state police operated under civil service arrangements; the townships did not. All four agencies operated in a "good government" political climate that placed a high value on the separation of electoral politics from the routine operation of the department by professional administrators.

State police service to College and Harris townships   Before the study, elected officials in both College and Harris townships had publicly explored the possibility of not renewing their contracts with State College and asking the state police to provide all police services. Through their task force participation, the state police prepared a number of proposals to serve various combinations of all Centre Region townships. Only state police service to College and Harris townships, however, was given serious consideration. The state police already served areas adjacent to these two townships. To serve the College and Harris areas, the state police proposed to reorganize the station's existing patrol zones, creating a new one for College and incorporating Harris into a zone that included an adjacent township outside the Centre Region. Each zone would have one patrol officer assigned around the clock and an investigator for follow-up investigations from 8 A.M. to midnight for both zones combined.

The proposed arrangements between the townships and the state police were the same as those used by the agency throughout the state. All services were to be provided without charge to the municipalities. The state police station commander and his superior were formally accountable to the agency's headquarters, not to the municipalities. However, it was common practice for station commanders to communicate as needed with local officials on matters of local concern and to be as accommodating as possible within the organization's rules and policies. One of the principal limitations in this regard was the agency's statewide policy of *not* enforcing local ordinances. However, if violation of a local ordinance could also be construed as a violation of state law (e.g., a noise ordinance violation might also constitute a disorderly conduct misdemeanor), the state police could be responsive by enforcing the state law.

Consolidation of the Patton and Ferguson departments   Two options were given serious consideration: (1) the merger of the existing Patton and Ferguson departments into one consolidated department to serve both townships and (2) the merger and expansion of these two eight-officer departments to serve Harris and College townships in addition to Patton and Ferguson. The two-township merger would yield a sworn force of sixteen; the four-township merger would result in a twenty-six-officer department, requiring the addition of ten officers to the current complements of the two township departments. In both options, the full-time equivalent of 1.5 civilians would be assigned to the department; and the administrative/supervisory hierarchy would consist of one chief in a full-time administrative capacity, one sergeant, and three corporals (providing shift supervision). In addition, in both options one of the sworn rank-and-file would serve full time as a criminal investigator.

The consolidated department would provide twenty-four-hour service to all areas and would determine the specific allocation of resources on the basis of standard professional criteria (calls for service, reported crime, response time). The police station would be located at the Ferguson Township municipal building. There was little difference in salaries, benefits, and personnel practices between the two existing agencies; under the proposal they would remain largely the same, with all pay and benefit differences resolved in favor of the higher levels. The chief's position would be open to all qualified applicants. Officers currently holding supervisory positions would be guaranteed the rank of corporal in the new department. A policy-making body consisting of all elected township supervisors representing the participating municipalities was to designate a civilian management board to fulfill the administrative oversight functions currently performed by township managers. The annual budget for the consolidated two-township department would be virtually identical to the combined budgets of the existing departments, whereas some economies of scale were estimated for the four-township option (an 11 percent reduction in per-officer costs from the cost of the two-township option). The allocation of costs among participating municipalities was not part of the study's responsibilities, although for illustrative purposes, the task force assumed that costs would be distributed according to current levels of demand as reflected in calls for service.

Total municipal consolidation   Yet another option required the merger of all three existing municipal departments (State College, Patton, and Ferguson) into one organization to serve all five municipalities (State College, Patton, Ferguson, College, and Harris). The new force would have 66 full-time sworn personnel, 14 full-time civilians, and 23 part-time civilians. The department's structure would be similar to that existing in the borough of State College, although the proportion of sworn personnel committed to full-time administrative/supervisory assignments would increase substantially, from 15 to 24 percent. As with the borough's arrangement, there would be three supervisory ranks below the level of chief, although a new rank of captain would be created and the rank of corporal eliminated. The proportion of officers committed to specialist (nonpatrol) assignments would remain stable at 18 percent. These changes would bring substantial differences in vertical and horizontal organizational segmentation to the citizens currently being served by the two largely undifferentiated Ferguson and Patton township departments. The consolidated department would have headquarters at the borough's municipal building.

All sworn and civilian personnel currently assigned to existing departments would be guaranteed positions in the consolidated department. The borough's existing civil service system would serve as the model for the new department, but township officers failing to meet civil service personnel standards would be given a one-time waiver at the time of consolidation. Supervisory officers in existing departments would be guaranteed supervisory ranks in the new department roughly commensurate with existing spans of control. Competition for the chief's position would be open to all qualified applicants. Pay and benefits for the new department would be modeled on the borough's plan, whose pay and benefits level were higher than those of the townships. All employees who became integrated into the consolidated department would be guaranteed levels of pay and pensions not less than those currently received.

The COG instructed the task force not to propose arrangements for the civilian oversight of the department, feeling that it was a political issue better left to elected officials to resolve. Informally, most members of the task force assumed that arrangements would be similar to those proposed for the township consolidation option. The total annual budget of the consolidated department was estimated to be virtually the same as the combined cost of the existing arrangements. Increases in salary and pension expenses were expected to be offset by reductions in the duplication of physical plant and equipment as well as by economies of scale in purchasing. The task force estimated the allocation of costs among participating municipalities on the same basis as for the township consolidation plan.

The Centre Region policy decision

At the time of this writing, police service delivery in the Centre Region has changed very little. Several proposals for increased coordination and functional consolidation of recordkeeping (by contract) have been implemented, but the same fundamental structure for direct services remains. The consolidation issue has not died but continues to be a topic of public discussion. The townships in particular have explored a variety of consolidation and contracting alternatives to existing arrangements, conducting both in-house and additional external studies. College Township is considering the feasibility of forming its own department. COG officials are discussing the advisability of pursuing regional consolidation of all municipal government services under one authority. In the future, some form of consolidation may take place, but the municipalities' decisions *not* to alter the existing arrangements after the work of the task force can shed light on why police agency consolidation occurs so rarely and what conditions make it more likely.

The Centre Region situation seems close to ideal in terms of the *feasibility* of consolidation. All of the service providers under consideration enjoy sound reputations as professionally competent departments. The communities—although somewhat different in size—are remarkably similar in social makeup and economy, in comparison with many other metropolitan areas. The existing departments enjoy cordial interagency relations. The members of the task force devoted a great deal of time to the proposals and worked together with an obvious commitment to producing the best possible administratively feasible proposals. Although some intergovernmental tension existed between the borough and the townships, the ongoing COG cooperative arrangement for the joint provision of other services shows that this tension can be overcome. Furthermore, no active coalition has arisen in any jurisdiction to oppose the *principle* of police agency consolidation. In fact, elected officials remain interested in pursuing this option.

Why then has there been no change? Many proponents of consolidation argue that the failure to consolidate is usually due to the inability of local politicians to resolve differences and give up control over one of the largest components of local government. According to this view, increased efficiency and professionalism are sacrificed to petty politics. This argument may apply marginally to the Centre Region, but for the most part, the communities of the Centre Region practice rational policy making.

Let us begin the analysis by making some assumptions to frame the decision-making process in this case. The first assumption is that the primary obligation of the elected officials of the municipalities is to best represent the interests of their constituents. Although compromise is a political necessity, officials cannot be expected to embrace changes that will work counter to the interests of their communities. The second assumption is that all decisionmakers had similar concerns about police service delivery (e.g., quality, quantity, cost, local control); this was revealed during their open discussions; however, it cannot be assumed that these concerns were weighted the same from one jurisdiction to the next. Third, it is reasonable to assume that the Centre Region decisionmakers operated with the same information about the content and consequences of the proposals, because police chiefs and managers from all municipalities were heavily involved in the task force, and the detailed study report was delivered to all elected officials, the press, and relevant appointed officials. Given these assumptions, it is possible to analyze the relative merits of the options and to see that none of the alternatives was preferable to enough of the jurisdictions to make a compromise possible.

The concerns of Centre Region decisionmakers can be divided into four categories: quality of service, quantity of service, cost, and local political control. In the following discussion, these criteria are used to compare existing arrangements with four of the most seriously considered consolidation options: (1) state police service to College and Harris townships, (2) consolidation of the Patton and Ferguson departments, (3) consolidation of police services to Patton, Ferguson, Harris, and College townships, and (4) consolidation of the police services of all townships and the borough into one agency (total municipal consolidation). The task force and the consultant provided information that allowed elected officials to compare the options on the four criteria.

Quality of service   Quality of police service is undoubtedly the most difficult of the four criteria to judge, yet it never became an issue among members of the task force or among local officials in subsequent public discussion. For many police professionals, quality of service delivery is equated with the capacity to reduce crime and apprehend offenders. However, the capacity of the police to reduce crime has not been well established in scientific research, and using arrest and clearance rates as indicators of police performance is fraught with measurement problems.[14] More important, no body of research exists that permits any reasonable inferences about the impact of various structural arrangements on crime and arrest rates in general, much less in the Centre Region. Aware of these facts, members of the task force relied on other indicators of service quality: the level of officer education and training; department reputation for honest, courteous, and caring service; and competent leadership. Although there were some differences in the levels of training provided by the four existing departments, all enjoyed strong reputations as professional agencies. A survey of citizens who had recently requested service from these departments revealed uniformly high evaluations of the officer's handling of the incident. Indeed, the public officials expressing the most interest in alternative arrangements had also indicated that the quality of service was not an issue. Because the various consolidation options did not appear likely to alter the quality of police services in ways that could be readily measured, this criterion did not become an important factor in decision making.

Quantity, cost, and local control of services   The task force was able to make fairly detailed estimates of the quantity and cost of police services under the various arrangements. Table 2 shows the average number of nonsupervisory officers providing direct service under each arrangement. Table 3 shows the annual cost per officer to each jurisdiction under the various arrangements. Table 4 offers an estimate of local control under each option.

These tables make several things clear. First, for any given criterion, the preferability of a given option varies from jurisdiction to jurisdiction. For example, considering the average number of direct-service officers on duty (Table 2), existing arrangements are the highest for State College and Ferguson townships but lowest for Harris Township. In terms of cost per officer, the best option for State College (total municipal consolidation) is the worst one for all the other jurisdictions. In terms of local control, total municipal

Table 2. Average number of direct-service officers on duty.

Option	State College	College	Harris	Ferguson	Patton
		Jurisdiction receiving service			
Existing arrangement	6.2	1.2	0.5	1.4	1.4
State police service to College and Harris	—	1.5	0.6	—	—
Two-township consolidation	—	—	—	1.2	1.3
Four-township consolidation	—	1.5	0.3	1.1	1.3
Total municipal consolidation	6.2	1.4	0.3	1.0	1.2

Note: Direct services are patrol, investigations, and crime prevention. Averages are based on a standard that the equivalent of one officer's 24-hour service requires 5.2 full-time equivalent officers. Officers are allocated according to annual levels of calls for service.

Table 3. Annual cost per officer (in $1,000).

Option	State College	College	Harris	Ferguson	Patton
		Jurisdiction receiving service			
Existing arrangement	40	33	32	37	34
State police service to College and Harris	—	0	0	—	—
Two-township consolidation	—	—	—	36	36
Four-township consolidation	—	32	32	32	32
Total municipal consolidation	38	38	38	38	38

Table 4. Local control of police services.

Option	State College	College	Harris	Ferguson	Patton
		Jurisdiction receiving service			
Existing arrangement	100	0	0	100	100
State police service to College and Harris	—	0	0	—	—
Two-township consolidation	—	—	—	50	50
Four-township consolidation	—	25	13	31	31
Total municipal consolidation	59	10	5	13	13

Note: Figures in the table represent the percentage of representatives in the policy-making body of elected officials who are from the specified jurisdiction receiving service. Figures for municipal consolidation alternatives presume representation proportional to population size. Under the state police arrangement, there is no formal provision for local jurisdiction policy making. Under the existing contract arrangement between State College and the two townships, there is no formal provision for policy making, although the townships can exert some control over the level of police service delivery and overall cost to the township by negotiating the terms of the contract.

consolidation is the second most preferable alternative for State College, College, and Harris but is the least preferable option for Ferguson and Patton.

The tables also show that for any given jurisdiction, no single alternative is clearly preferable across all three criteria. Table 5 summarizes the trade-offs among the three criteria for each jurisdiction, focusing on the highest-ranking option in each category. If existing arrangements were changed, for example, the best option for State College would be total municipal consolidation. That option would result in a 5 percent reduction in cost per officer (as calculated from the data in Table 3) but at a considerable loss of local control of service delivery. As calculated from data in Tables 2 and 3, Patton and Ferguson could achieve 6 and 14 percent improvements, respectively, in cost efficiency by consolidating with the other two townships but could expect to experience 7 and 21 percent reductions, respectively, in level of direct service and a substantial reduction in degree of local control. College and Harris obviously had the most to gain by a change in existing arrangements. The State Police option was clearly preferable in terms of cost efficiency for both and offered a substantial increase in service level for Harris. However, this option ranked well below the others on local control, at least a degree of which was available under existing arrangements through contract negotiations. Harris and College township officials had made public statements over the years about the desirability of some intertownship arrangement, and they had actively pursued alternatives to existing arrangements. Thus, they appeared open to some form of arrangement with the other two townships. But neither Ferguson nor Patton township had found it to *its* advantage to enter into such an arrangement.

Table 5. Tradeoffs among service level, cost efficiency, and local control.

| | Jurisdiction receiving service | | | | |
Criterion	State College	College	Harris	Ferguson	Patton
Service level	A/E	B/D	B	A	A
Cost efficiency	E	B	B	D	D
Local control	A	D	D	A	A

Note: Each letter in the table represents the most favorable option for the
  criterion specified. Two letters in a cell indicate a tie.

A—Existing arrangements
B—State police service to College and Harris
C—Two-township consolidation
D—Four-township consolidation
E—Total municipal consolidation

Of course, choosing among options is more complex than simply identifying the most desirable alternatives. Although compromises are always theoretically possible, the benefits of the various options were distributed so differently from one jurisdiction to another that it was unlikely that compromises acceptable to two or more jurisdictions could be found. It is hardly surprising, then, that no fundamental organizational changes were made in the Centre Region.

Consolidation may not be forever infeasible among Centre Region jurisdictions, but it will be necessary to formulate new alternatives that are more attractive than existing arrangements. The areas with the most potential for change are cost efficiency and local control. For example, the cost of total consolidation was unattractive to the townships because in all cases it represented an increase from existing arrangements—as much as 19 percent for Harris Township. The way to substantially decrease cost per officer is to reduce the number of sworn officers in the consolidated force.[15] Not filling vacancies during an interim period before consolidation and not expanding the force as the population of the serviced jurisdictions grows are two ways of reducing the force. Of course, this assumes that quantity and quality of service would not be affected by such reductions. Perhaps a consolidated organization would have greater flexibility in responding to service demands and consequently be more efficient, but that is not clear from the proposals generated thus far.

Dealing with the loss of local control over police is probably the greatest challenge in making change more attractive to most of these municipalities. The state police could enhance their responsiveness to local concerns by enforcing local ordinances and providing formal channels through which local officials could communicate their views on service delivery. These measures, however, would complicate the organization's capacity to provide centralized direction to its widely dispersed stations and would make uniform procedures difficult to implement. The principal difficulty inherent in the various forms of municipal consolidation is finding a politically palatable way to soften the accompanying loss of local control. State College's concern over the existing arrangements is that despite its having the clear majority of the Centre Region's residential population and paying by far the largest contribution to fund COG services, the borough has no greater voting power than each of the much smaller townships. Some borough officials have publicly contemplated leaving the COG if this arrangement is not changed. On the other hand, the townships fear that if representation on a policy-making police board were to be allocated on a population basis, the borough's interests would always prevail. A workable compromise might give the borough a clear plurality—short of a majority—on the board, which would enable the townships to outvote the borough but only with a unanimous vote.

Ironically, with the important exception of the budget, the elected officials of these municipalities did not exert much direct influence at the time of this case over police policy and operations, matters left mostly to appointed administrators. To the extent that the principal policy-making function of these officials vis-à-vis the police is to determine the cost and overall level of service their communities receive, another option is to create a single consolidated police force that provides service at the same unit cost to each municipality on a separate contract basis. The department would be overseen by a board of elected officials representing each jurisdiction, each having the same number of votes but having the discretion to decide annually the level of service it wished to purchase.[16] Its principal drawback is the need for stability or for only small annual changes in overall service levels contracted by participating municipalities.

Compromise might also be possible if a persuasive case could be made for the long-term benefits of consolidation. Some proponents of total municipal consolidation have argued that consolidated service delivery provides a more attractive environment for economic development in the region. They reason, further, that a consolidated regional government would exercise greater clout in state politics and therefore encourage policies more favorable to the region. Others have suggested that it would be in the borough's interest to make short-term compromises attractive to the townships in order to obtain the long-term benefit of influencing regional policies— particularly because townships are likely to be the areas of greatest regional economic and demographic growth for several decades. The difficulties with the long-term, big-picture perspective are that (1) the hypothetical benefits are far from certain, and (2) local decisionmakers—like those at the state and national levels—tend to be most influenced by the short-term implications of policy choices.

Conclusion

The body of research on police consolidation suggests that local policymakers would be unwise to assume a *prima facie* case either in favor of or opposed to consolidation. The Centre Region's experience with the consolidation issue suggests that it is possible to gather evidence on the likely impact of a variety of structural arrangements for police service delivery and to make rational choices about them. Although the Centre Region had many characteristics that seemed to make it an attractive candidate for consolidation, a careful analysis of the evidence indicates that each alternative to existing arrangements failed to offer sufficient benefits to enough jurisdictions to make change desirable and hence politically feasible.

How does one find common ground among political actors whose separate interests are not equally served by any given arrangement? In this case, change is rational only if the circumstances of these jurisdictions change in a way that either makes their interests converge or makes compromise more attractive. Where interests or priorities differ, crises are most likely to be the impetus for changes of the magnitude required for consolidation. The most likely source of crisis in police agencies is either fiscal disaster (a government's inability to support its department) or scandal (widespread corruption or misconduct). The causes of these problems might be unrelated to the structure of existing arrangements, but under such circumstances, the benefits of consolidation in one form or another might become obvious, and the pressure for immediate action might be so great that previously unacceptable compromises would become possible. In the absence of emergency conditions, however, policymakers need not view the failure to consolidate as a victory for irrational "political considerations." A careful analysis of the local circumstances may simply show that consolidation is not the best choice.

1. President's Commission on Law Enforcement and Administration of Justice, *The Challenge of Crime in a Free Society* (Washington, D.C.: U.S. Government Printing Office, 1967).

2. Daniel L. Skoler, *Organizing the Non-System: Governmental Structuring of Criminal Justice Systems* (Lexington, Mass.: D.C. Heath & Co., 1977).

3. Daniel L. Skoler, "Police Consolidation and Coordination," in Richard A. Staufenberger, ed., *Progress in Policing: Essays on Change* (Cambridge, Mass.: Ballinger Publishing Co., 1980), 103–128.

4. Lori M. Henderson, "Intergovernmental Service Arrangements and the Transfer of Functions," in *The Municipal Year Book* (Washington, D.C.: International City Management Association, 1985), 194–202.

5. Peter W. Colby, "Intergovernmental Contracting for Police Services," *Journal of Police Science and Administration* 10(1980):36.

6. Skoler, *Organizing the Non-System*, 85.

7. G. J. Skoien and M. Vernick, "Evaluation of Police Contracting—A Case Study of the Village of Dexter (MI)" (Ann Arbor: University of Michigan Institute of Public Policy Studies, 1977).

8. Peter W. Colby and S. L. Mehay, "Intergovernmental Contracting for Municipal Police Services—An Empirical Analysis," *Land Economics* 55(1979):59–72.

9. Elinor Ostrom, Roger B. Parks, and Gordon P. Whitaker, *Patterns of Metropolitan Policing* (Cambridge, Mass.: Ballinger Publishing Co., 1978).

10. Roger B. Parks and Elinor Ostrom, "Complex Models of Urban Service Systems," in Terry N. Clark, ed., *Urban Policy Analysis: Directions for Future Research*, Urban Affairs Annual Reviews, vol. 21 (Beverly Hills, Calif.: Sage Publications, 1981):171–199.

11. For a review of these studies, see

Vincent Ostrom, Robert Bish, and Elinor Ostrom, *Local Government in the United States* (San Francisco: ICS Press, 1988), and Roger B. Parks, "Using Sample Surveys to Compare Police Performance" (Bloomington: Indiana University Workshop in Political Theory and Policy Analysis, 1980).

12. Brian Stipak, "Citizen Satisfaction with Urban Services: Potential Misuse as a Performance Indicator," *Public Administration Review* (January/February, 1979):46–52; Harry Pachon and Nicholas P. Lovrich, Jr., "The Consolidation of Urban Public Services: A Focus on the Police," *Public Administration Review* 37(1977):38–47; and Nicholas P. Lovrich, Jr., "Scale and Performance in Governmental Operations: An Empirical Assessment of Public Choice Assumptions," *Public Administration Quarterly* 9(1985): 165–195.

13. Stephen D. Mastrofski, "Policing the Beat: The Impact of Organizational Scale on Patrol Officer Behavior in Urban Residential Neighborhoods," *Journal of Criminal Justice* 9(1981):343–358

14. Gordon P. Whitaker, Stephen Mastrofski, Elinor Ostrom, Roger B. Parks, and Stephen L. Percy, *Basic Issues in Police Performance* (Washington, D.C.: U.S. Department of Justice, 1982).

15. Some reduction could also be achieved by setting salaries and benefits at a lower level, but this would raise another set of sticky political problems and undoubtedly result in legal action by the borough's bargaining unit.

16. This is the system employed by the York County, Pennsylvania, Regional Police Force.

PART 2

Accomplishing the
Police Mission

Crime and Policing

Mark H. Moore,
Robert C. Trojanowicz, and George L. Kelling

The core mission of the police is to control crime. No one disputes this. Indeed, professional crime fighting enjoys wide public support as the basic strategy of policing precisely because it embodies a deep commitment to this objective. In contrast, other proposed strategies such as problem-solving or community policing appear on the surface to blur this focus.[1] If these strategies were to leave the community more vulnerable to criminal victimization, they would be undesirable alternatives. In judging the value of alternative police strategies in controlling crime, however, one should not be misled by rhetoric or mere expressed commitment to the goal; one must keep one's eye on demonstrated effectiveness in achieving the goal.

Professional crime-fighting now relies predominantly on three tactics: (1) motorized patrol; (2) rapid response to calls for service; and (3) retrospective investigation of crimes.[2] Over the past few decades, police responsiveness has been enhanced by connecting police to citizens by telephones, radios, and cars, and by matching police officer schedules and locations to anticipated calls for service.[3] The police focus on serious crime has also been sharpened by screening calls for service, targeting patrol, and developing forensic technology (e.g., automated fingerprint systems, computerized criminal record files, etc.).[4]

Although these tactics have scored their successes, they have

Reprinted from the June 1988 issue of *Perspectives on Policing*, a publication of the National Institute of Justice, U.S. Department of Justice, Washington, D.C., and the Program in Criminal Justice Policy and Management, John F. Kennedy School of Government, Harvard University. Points of view or opinions expressed in the publication are those of the authors and do not necessarily represent the official position or policies of the U.S. Department of Justice.

been criticized within and outside policing for being reactive rather than proactive. They have also been criticized for failing to prevent crime.[5]

Reactive tactics have some virtues, of course. The police go where crimes have occurred and when citizens have summoned them; otherwise, they do not intrude. The police keep their distance from the community, and thereby retain their impartiality. They do not develop the sorts of relationships with citizens that could bias their responses to crime incidents. These are virtues insofar as they protect citizens from an overly intrusive, too familiar police.

Moreover, the reactive tactics do have preventive effects—at least in theory. The prospect of the police arriving at a crime in progress as a result of a call or a chance observation is thought to deter crimes.[6] The successful prosecution of offenders (made possible by retrospective investigation) is also thought to deter offenders.[7] And even if it does not deter, a successfully prosecuted investigation incapacitates criminals who might otherwise go on to commit other crimes.[8]

Finally, many police forces have developed proactive tactics to deal with crime problems that could not be handled through conventional reactive methods. In drug dealing, organized crime, and vice enforcement, for example, where no immediate victims exist to mobilize the police, the police have developed special units which rely on informants, covert surveillance, and undercover investigations rather than responses to calls for service.[9] In the area of juvenile offenses where society's stake in preventing crimes seems particularly great, the police have created athletic leagues, formed partnerships with schools to deal with drug abuse and truancy, and so on.[10] It is not strictly accurate, then, to characterize modern policing as entirely reactive.

Still, the criticism of the police as being too reactive has some force. It is possible that the police could do more to control serious crime than they now achieve. Perhaps research will yield technological breakthroughs that will dramatically improve the productivity of police investigation. For now, however, the greatest potential for improved crime control may not lie in the continued enhancement of response times, patrol tactics, and investigative techniques. Rather, improved crime control can be achieved by (1) diagnosing and managing problems in the community that produce serious crimes; (2) fostering closer relations with the community to facilitate crime solving; and (3) building self-defense capabilities within the community itself. Among the results may be increased apprehension of criminals. To the extent that problem-solving or community strategies of policing direct attention to and prepare the police to exploit local knowledge and capacity to control crime, they will be useful to the future of policing. To explore these possibilities, this article examines what is known about serious crime: what it is, where and how it occurs, and natural points of intervention. Current and proposed police tactics are then examined in light of what is known about their effectiveness in fighting serious crime.

Serious crime

To individual citizens, a serious crime is an offense that happened to *them*. That is why police departments throughout the country are burdened with calls requesting responses to offenses that the police regard as minor. While there are reasons to take such calls seriously, there is also the social and administrative necessity to weigh the relative gravity of the offenses. Otherwise, there is no principle for apportioning society's indignation and determination to punish; nor is there any basis for rationing police responses. The concept of serious crime, then, is necessarily a *social* judgment—not an individual one. Moreover, it is a *value* judgment—not simply a technical issue. The question of what constitutes serious crime is resolved formally by the criminal code. But the criminal code often fails to give precise guidance to police administrators who must decide which crimes to emphasize. They need some concept that distinguishes the offenses that properly outrage the citizenry and require extended police attention from the many lesser offenses that pose less urgent threats to society.

Like many things that require social value judgments, the issue of what constitutes serious crime is badly neglected.[11] Rather than face a confusing public debate, society relies on convention, or administrative expertise, or some combination of the two, to set standards. Yet, if we are to assess and improve police practice in dealing with serious crime, it is necessary to devote some thought to the question of what constitutes serious crime.

Defining serious crime   The usual view of serious crime emphasizes three characteristics of offenses. The most important is physical violence or violation. Death, bloody wounds, crippling injuries, even cuts and bruises increase the severity of a crime.[12] Sexual violation also has a special urgency.[13] Crime victims often suffer property losses as well as pain and violation. Economic losses count in reckoning the seriousness of an offense. Still, society generally considers physical attacks—sexual and nonsexual—as far more serious than attacks on property.[14]

A second feature of serious crime concerns the size of the victim's losses. A robbery resulting in a murder or a permanent, disfiguring injury is considered worse than one that produces only cuts, bruises, and fears. An armored car heist netting millions is considered more serious than a purse-snatching yielding the price of a junkie's next fix.

Third, the perceived seriousness of an offense is influenced by the relationship between offenders and victims. Commonly, crimes against strangers are viewed as more serious than crimes committed in the context of ongoing relationships.[15] The reason is partly that the threat to society from indiscriminate predators is more far-reaching than the threat from offenders who limit their targets to spouses, lovers, and friends. Moreover, society judges the evil intent of the offender to be more evident in crimes against strangers. In these crimes, there are no chronic grievances or provocations in the background to raise the issue of who attacked whom first and in what way. The crime is an out-and-out attack, not a mere dispute.[16]

These characteristics—violence, significant losses to victims, predatory strangers—capture much of what is important to societal and police images of serious crime. The intuitive appeal of these criteria is reflected in the categories of the FBI's Uniform Crime Reports. Murder, rape, robbery, burglary, aggravated assault, and auto theft (most presumably committed by strangers) are prominently reported as Part I offenses. This key national account of crimes not only reflects, but anchors society's view of serious crime as predatory street crime.

While this notion has the sanction of intuitive appeal, convention, and measurement, it also contains subtle biases which, once pointed out, might cause society and the police to adjust their traditional views. First, the accepted image of crime seems to downplay the importance of crime committed in the context of ongoing relationships. From the perspective of the general citizenry, such offenses seem less important because they do not pose a *general* threat to society. From the perspective of the police (and other criminal justice officials), such crimes are less clear-cut because the existence of the prior relationship muddies the distinction between offender and victim and increases the likelihood that a case will be dropped when the antagonists resolve the dispute that produced the offense.

From the victim's point of view, however, the fact of a relationship to the offender dramatically intensifies the seriousness of the offense. A special terror arises when one is locked into an abusive relationship with a spouse or lover. A date that turns into a rape poisons a victim's psyche much more than an attack by a stranger. And, as Boston Police Commissioner Mickey Roache found when he was heading a unit dealing with interracial violence in Boston, serious interracial intimidation and violence did not appear in crime reports as robberies or burglaries. Rather, the serious crimes appeared as vandalism. What made the vandalism terrifying was that it was directed at the same address night after night.

Second, the view of serious crime as predatory violence tends to obscure the importance of fear as a separate, pernicious aspect of the crime problem. To a degree, the issue of fear is incorporated in the conventional view of serious crime. Indeed, fear is what elevates predatory street crimes above crimes that occur within personal relationships. What the conventional view misses, however, is the empirical fact that minor offenses and incivilities trigger citizens' fears more than actual crime victimization. Rowdy youth, abandoned cars, and graffiti frighten people, force them to restrict their movements, and motivate them to buy guns, locks and dogs. To the extent that the conventional view of serious crime deflects attention from fear and the offenses that stimulate fear, it may obscure an important opportunity for the police to contribute to the solution of the serious crime problem.

Third, defining serious crime in terms of the absolute magnitude of material losses to victims (without reference to the victim's capacity to absorb the loss, or the implications of the loss for people other than the victim) introduces the potential for injustice and ineffectiveness in targeting police attention. In the conventional view, a jewel theft at a swank hotel attracts more attention than the mugging of an elderly woman for her Social Security check. Yet it is clear that the stolen Social Security check represents a larger portion of the elderly woman's wealth than the losses to the hotel's well-insured customers. The robbery of a federally insured bank would attract more attention than the robbery of an inner-city convenience store. But the robbery of the ghetto store could end the entrepreneurial career of the owner, drive the store from the area, and, with the store's departure, deprive the neighborhood of one of its few social underpinnings.

Fourth, to the extent that the conventional view of crime emphasizes the reality of individual criminal victimization, it underplays crimes that have symbolic significance. The current emphasis on child sexual abuse, for example, is important in part because it sustains a broad social commitment to the general care and protection of children. The current emphasis on domestic assault, among other things, helps to sustain a normative movement that is changing the status of women in marriages. The interest in white-collar economic crimes and political corruption can be explained by the desire to set higher standards for the conduct of those in powerful positions. The social response to these offenses is important because it strengthens, or redefines, broad social norms.

In sum, the view of crime as predatory, economically significant violence stresses the substantial losses associated with street offenses. It obscures the losses to society that result from offenses that poison relationships, transform neighborhoods into isolated camps, and undermine important social institutions. It misses the terror of the abused spouse or molested child, the wide social consequences of driving merchants out of business, the rot that drug dealing brings to an urban community, and the polarizing effects of fear. An alternative view of serious crime would be one that acknowledged violence as a key component of serious crime but added the issues of safety within relationships, the importance of fear, and the extent to which offenses collapse individual lives and social institutions as well as inflict individual losses. This enlarged conception rests on the assumption that the police can and should defend more social terrain than the streets. Their challenge is to preserve justice and order within the institutions of the community.

Levels, trends, and social location of serious crime   It is no simple matter to represent the current levels, recent trends, and social location of serious crime. Still, several important observations can be made.

First, in any year, a noticeable fraction of American households is touched by serious crime. In 1986, 5 percent of American households experienced the violence associated with a rape, robbery, or assault. Almost 8 percent of households were touched by at least one serious crime: rape, robbery, aggravated assault, or burglary.[17] When considering the likelihood that a household will be victimized sometime in the next 5 years, these figures increase dramatically, for a household faces these risks *each year*. Thus, most American households have first- or second-hand experience with serious crime.

Second, from the mid-1960s to the mid-1970s, the United States experienced a dramatic increase in the level of serious crime. In fact, the level of serious crime reached historic highs. Since the mid-seventies, the level of serious crime has remained approximately constant, or declined slightly.[18]

Third, criminal victimization is disproportionately concentrated among minority and poor populations in the United States. Homicide is the leading cause of death for young minority males living in metropolitan areas.[19] Black households are victimized by violent crimes such as robbery, rape, and aggravated assault at one and a half times the frequency of white families. The poor are victimized at one and a half times the rate of the wealthy.[20] These numbers probably underestimate the real differences in the losses—material and psychological—experienced by rich and poor victims, since those who are black and poor have fewer resources to deal with the losses associated with victimization.

Precipitating causes of serious crime   In searching for ways to prevent or control serious crime, the police look for precipitating causes. While it may be useful to examine what some call the root causes of crime (e.g., social injustice, unequal economic opportunity, poor schooling, weak family structures, or mental illness), such things are relatively unimportant from a police perspective since the police exercise little influence over them.[21] The police operate on the surface of social life. They must handle incidents, situations, and people as they are now—not societies or people as they might have been. For these reasons, the immediately precipitating causes of serious crime are far more important to the police than are broader questions about the root causes of crime. Four precipitating causes of crime seem relevant to policing: (1) dangerous people; (2) criminogenic situations; (3) alcohol and drug use; and (4) frustrating relationships.

Dangerous people   One way the police view serious crime is to see the precipitating cause in the character of the offender. A crime occurs when a predatory offender finds a victim. One could reduce such events by teaching potential victims to avoid situations and behaviors that make them vulnerable. And, to some degree, the police do this. But the far more common and attractive path for controlling predatory crime is to identify and apprehend the predators. Thus, dangerous offenders can be seen as a precipitating cause of serious crime and an important focus of police attention.[22]

Recent research on criminal careers provides a firm empirical basis for this view.[23] Interviews with convicted criminals conducted by the Rand Corporation indicate that some criminal offenders committed crimes very frequently and sustained this activity over a long career.[24] Moreover, these violent predators accounted for a substantial amount of the serious crime.[25] Now, an investigation of the root causes of such patterns of offending might disclose strong influences of social disadvantage and psychological maltreatment in shaping the personalities of such offenders. Moreover, the influence of these factors might reasonably mitigate their guilt. One might also hold out some hope for their future rehabilitation (through the natural process of aging if nothing else). So, the criminal proclivities of violent predators need not be viewed as either inevitable or unchangeable. From the vantage point of the police, however, the presence of such offenders in the community can reasonably be viewed as an important precipitating cause of crime. Controlling such offenders through incapacitation or close surveillance thus becomes an important crime control strategy.

Having noted the role of dangerous offenders in producing serious crime, it is worth emphasizing that such offenders account for only a portion of the total amount of serious crime—far more than their share, but still only about half of all serious crime.[26] The necessary conclusion is that a significant portion of the serious crime problem cannot be attributed to determined attacks by career criminals or to predatory offenders. These crimes arise from quite different causes.

Criminogenic situations   Some of these crimes might be produced by situational effects. Darkness and congestion around a subway exit may create an attractive location for muggings. An after-hours bar may host more than its share of fights. A rock house from which crack is being sold may become a magnet for violence. Closing time in a popular disco may produce fights among teenagers leaving the scene. In sum, there are some places, times, and activities that bring people together in ways that increase the likelihood of serious crime.

The fact that this occurs is knowable to police. By analyzing calls for service, they can observe that there are repeated calls made from certain places and at certain times.[27] These "hot spots" become important targets of police attention.[28] For example, patrol units might be dispatched just to sit and observe at the appropriate times. There may also be other solutions including permanent changes in the criminogenic situations. For example, the subway area could be lighted; the attention of a neighborhood watch group could be directed to the troublespot; the after-hours bar could be put out of business; aggressive street-level enforcement could be directed against the rock house; or transportation could be arranged for the kids leaving the disco so the crowd thins out more quickly.[29]

Alcohol and drug use   Crimes are also significantly related to alcohol or drug abuse.[30] It is now quite clear that: (1) a surprisingly high percentage of those arrested for serious crimes are drug or alcohol users;[31] (2) many offenders have drunk alcohol or taken drugs prior to committing crimes;[32] and (3) victims as well as offenders are often intoxicated or under the influence of drugs.[33] What is unclear is exactly how alcohol and drugs produce their criminogenic effect. Four hypotheses have been advanced to explain this phenomenon.[34]

The first is that physiological effects stimulate or license the person to commit crimes. The theory of stimulation may be appropriate to methamphetamines or PCP, which sometimes seem to produce violent reactions among consumers. The theory of licensing or disinhibition seems more appropriate in the case of alcohol where the release of inhibitions is arguably the mechanism that permits offenses to occur.[35]

Second, dependence or addiction forces users to spend more money on purchasing drugs, and they turn to crime in a desperate effort to maintain their habits. This is a powerful theory in the case of heroin (under conditions of prohibition), and perhaps for cocaine. It is far less powerful for alcohol or marijuana.

Third, drug use gradually demoralizes people by putting them on the wrong side of the law, bringing them into contact with criminals, and gradually weakening their commitment to the obligations of a civil society. Again, this seems more appropriate for those who become deeply involved with drugs and alcohol over a long period of time, and therefore relies more on the dependence-producing attributes of drugs rather than on the immediate intoxicating effects.

Fourth, intoxicated people make particularly good victims. In some cases, intoxication makes people vulnerable to victimization.[36] In other cases, it causes victims to provoke their attackers.[37] In either case, a serious crime can result.

Whichever theory, or theories, is correct, the close association among drugs, alcohol, and serious crime suggests that the amount of serious crime might be decreased by reducing levels of alcohol and drug use, or by identifying those offenders who use drugs intensively and reducing their consumption.[38]

Frustrating relationships   Finally, the fact that many serious offenses occur in the context of ongoing relationships suggests that some relationships may be criminogenic. Relationships can cause crime because they create expectations. If the expectations are not met, the resulting disappointment produces anger. Anger may lead to vengeance and retaliation. In such cycles, the question of who caused the ultimate crime becomes confused. Usually, the offender is the one least damaged after the fight. A court may conclude that the crime stemmed from the evil intentions of the person identified as the offender. But this may not be the best way to view the problem from the vantage point of crime control or crime prevention.

It might be more suitable to see the crimes as emerging from a set of relationships that are frustrating and provocative. The proper response might be to work on the relationship through mediation, restructuring, or dissolution. Indeed, this is often the challenge confronting the police when they encounter spouse abuse, child abuse, and other sorts of intrafamily violence. In such situations, arrests may be appropriate and effective in deterring future crime and in restructuring the relationship.[39] There are many other crimes which emerge from less obvious relationships: the personal relationships of neighbors and friends; the economic relations of landlord and tenant or employer and employee; or transient relations that last just long enough to provoke a quarrel or seed a grudge. Seen this way, many serious crimes—including murders, robberies, rapes, and burglaries—are disputes and grievances among people rather than criminal attacks.

Controlling serious crime

Currently the police fight serious crime by developing a capacity to intercept it—to be in the right place at the right time so that the crime is thwarted, or to arrive so quickly after the fact that the offender is caught. Reactive crime fighting is intuitively appealing to both the police and those to whom the police are accountable. It is unclear, however, whether the reactive response really works. Over the last two decades, confidence in the reactive approach has been eroded by the accumulation of empirical evidence suggesting that these tactics are of only limited effectiveness. It is not that the approach fails to control crime. (It would be foolish to imagine that levels of serious crime would stay the same if police patrols and investigations were halted.) Rather, the limits of the reactive strategy are now becoming apparent. Further gains in police effectiveness in dealing with serious crime must come from different approaches. Key research findings suggesting the limitations of the reactive approach are these.

First, the Kansas City Preventive Patrol Study found that levels of serious crime were not significantly influenced by doubling the number of cars patrolling the streets.[40] This cast doubt on the potential for reducing serious crime simply by increasing the level of preventive patrol.

Second, a study of the effectiveness of rapid response to calls for service (also in Kansas City) found that the probability of making an arrest for most serious crimes was unaffected by the speed with which the police responded. The crucial factor was not the speed of the police response, but the speed with which citizens raised the alarm. If citizens did not notice the crime, or did not call the police quickly, no amount of speed in the police response helped much.[41]

Third, studies of the investigative process revealed that the key factor in determining whether a crime was solved was the quality of the information contributed to the investigation by victims and witnesses about the identity of the offender.[42] If they could not be helpful, forensic wizardry generally was not up to solving the crime.

It is important to understand that these weaknesses appeared in precisely those areas of crime control where the reactive strategy should have been particularly strong: i.e., in dealing with crimes such as murder, rape, robbery, assault, and burglary. These crimes could be expected to produce alarms; they also were interceptable and solvable by a vigilant police force waiting to be mobilized by outraged citizens.

There are, of course, many other kinds of serious crimes for which the reactive police strategy is much more obviously inappropriate.[43] It cannot, for example, deal with consensual crimes such as drug dealing behind closed doors. Nor can it deal with crimes such as extortion and loan sharking where the victims are too afraid to report the crimes. A reactive strategy cannot deal with sophisticated white collar crimes or political corruption where the losses associated with the crimes are so widely distributed that people do not notice that they have been victimized. Finally, a reactive strategy cannot deal even with traditional street crimes in those parts of cities where confidence in the police has eroded to such a degree that the citizens no longer call when they are victimized.

Although these findings and intrinsic limitations of the reactive strategy have not unseated the intuitive appeal of and wide experience with the reactive crime fighting strategy, they have added to a growing sense of frustration within police departments. Confronted by high levels of crime and limited budgets, the police felt a growing need for initiative and thoughtfulness in tackling serious crime. Working within the logic of their current approaches, but reaching for additional degrees of effectiveness, during the 1970s the police developed new proactive tactics.

Developments in proactive crime fighting   To deal with serious street crime, the police developed the tactic of directed patrol. Sometimes these patrols were aimed at locations that seemed particularly vulnerable to crimes, such as branch banks, convenience stores, and crowded bars. Other times, the patrols were focused on individuals who, on the basis of past record or recent information, were thought to be particularly active offenders.[44]

The police sought to attack street robberies and muggings through anticrime squads that sent decoys into the streets to prompt active muggers into committing a crime in the full view of the police. The police also sought to control home robberies and burglaries through sting operations involving undercover officers who operated as fences to identify and gather evidence against the offenders.

Finally, the police sought to enhance the effective impact of their enforcement efforts by increasing the quality of the cases they made. Quality Investigation Programs[45] and Integrated Criminal Apprehension Programs[46] were adopted by many departments to increase the likelihood that arrests would be followed by conviction and long prison sentences.

For the most part, each of these innovations produced its successes. The perpetrator-oriented patrols, sting operations, and quality investigation efforts were a little more successful than the location-oriented directed patrols and undercover operations directed against street robbery. Nonetheless, the police did demonstrate that concentrated efforts could increase arrests, clearances, and convictions. These efforts did not show that these programs alone—without the support of courts and corrections and the involvement of the community—could reduce aggregate levels of serious crime in the cities in which they were tried.

Moreover, insofar as each program took a more aggressive and proactive approach to crime, it also troubled those who were concerned that the police not become too intrusive. Perpetrator-oriented patrols, for example, raised the question of whether it was appropriate to target offenders rather than offenses, and if so, on what evidentiary basis.[47] The use of undercover tactics to deal with both robbery and burglary raised important questions about entrapment.[48] And the emphasis on producing convictions from arrests prompted worries that the police might be motivated to manufacture as well as simply record and preserve evidence. Arguably, these civil liberties concerns were inappropriate at a time when the police seemed unable to deal with high crime rates. The fact that these concerns arose, however, indicated that the police were, in fact, using their authority more intensively than they had when they were relying principally on reactive strategies. Such concerns must be reckoned a cost of the new efforts.

The police also made substantial investments in their ability to deal with those crimes that could not be handled through routine patrol or investigative operations, either because the crimes were too complicated to handle with ordinary arrest and investigative methods, or because the routine operations would not disclose the crime. In terms of dealing with especially demanding crimes, like hostage takings or well-armed offenders, the police developed Special Weapons and Arrest Teams. They also enhanced their capacities to deal with riots and demonstrations. And at the other end of the spectrum, the police developed special procedures for dealing with deranged and disordered offenders who often looked violent (and sometimes were) but mostly were simply mentally disturbed.

To deal with crimes that were not always revealed through the ordinary procedures of complaints by victims and witnesses, the police developed special units skilled in investigating the sensitive areas of child sexual abuse, rape, and domestic assault. They also created special investigative units to deal with high-level drug dealing, organized crime, arson, and sophisticated frauds. These units often relied on special intelligence files as well as special investigative procedures, such as the recruitment of informants, electronic wiretaps, and sustained undercover investigations. These programs also scored their successes and enhanced the ability of the police to deal with serious crime.

Missed opportunities in crime fighting?   These innovations demonstrated the resourcefulness and creativity of the police as they faced the challenge of high crime rates with limited financial resources, diminished authority, and constrained managerial prerogatives. With the benefit of hindsight, however, some crucial oversights are apparent.

First, there was little appreciation of the crucial role that better information from the community would play in strengthening police performance.[49] It was not that the police were unaware of their dependency on citizens for information. Long before it was demonstrated that the success of rapid response to all crime calls and retrospective investigation depended on the willingness of victims and witnesses to report crimes and aid in their solution, the police had mounted campaigns mobilizing citizens to support their local police.

The real problem was that the police did not adequately consider what was needed to attract that support. They thought that their interest and ready availability would be sufficient. They did not understand that citizens felt vulnerable to retaliation by offenders in the community and needed a closer connection with the police if they were going to help them solve the crime. Nor did the police understand that a partnership with the community could be constructed only from the material of daily encounters with the public; in particular, by taking seriously the public's concern with less serious offenses. In short, while the police knew that they were dependent on the community for information about crime, they never asked the public what was needed to obtain help beyond setting up 911 systems.

Second, the police rarely looked behind an offense to its precipitating causes. Nor did they think about crime prevention in terms of managing the precipitating causes. They knew, of course, that much crime was being produced by dangerous offenders, criminogenic situations, alcohol and drug abuse, and aggravating relationships. But they were ambivalent about acting on that knowledge. They tended to limit their responsibilities to applying the law to incidents to which they were summoned; they did not think in terms of applying instruments of civil law or the capacities of other city agencies to work on the proximate causes of crime. Criminal investigations emphasized legal evidence of guilt or innocence—not the question of precipitating causes.

There were many reasons to maintain this narrow focus on law enforcement. To a degree, it protected police organizations from criticisms that they were lawless and out of control. The police could explain that they merely enforced the laws and that they exercised no discretion beyond this basic function. The narrow focus on law enforcement also protected the organization from failure in its basic crime control mission. If the police role was limited to applying the criminal law to offenses rather than to the more challenging goal of actually preventing and controlling crime, the police could succeed even if crime were not controlled. They could blame the other parts of the criminal justice system for their failures to deter and incapacitate the offenders whom the police had arrested. Finally, the narrow focus was consistent with the training and aspirations of the police themselves. Arresting people and using authority was real police work; mediating disputes, mobilizing communities, and badgering other city agencies for improved services was social work.

Whatever the reasons, the police remained reluctant to develop the internal capabilities needed to make their anecdotal impressions of precipitating causes systematic and powerful. Crime analysis sections merely kept statistics or characterized the location of crime; they did not identify dangerous offenders or trouble spots and avoided examining the role of alcohol and drugs in the serious crime problem. Nor did they propose alternative methods for dealing with crime problems. From the perspective of the police, it was far better to stay at the surface of social life and respond to crimes as they occurred rather than to intervene more widely and actively to manage the immediate conditions that were producing crimes.

Third, the police never fully exploited the self-defense capacities of the community itself. They did offer advice to merchants and citizen groups about how they could protect themselves from criminal victimization. And they helped organize neighborhood watch groups. But the main efforts went into helping the communities become more effective operational auxiliaries to the police departments. Citizens were encouraged to mark their property not only because it helped the police solve the crime, should the item be stolen, but also because it allowed the police to return the property to the owners. Crime watch groups were instructed to call the police rather than to intervene themselves. This was consistent with the desires of the police to maintain their monopoly on both expertise and operational capability in dealing with crime. They did not really want any growth in private security—whether it took the form of volunteer associations such as the Guardian Angels or commercial operations such as Burns Security Guards. Because of that interest, police commitment to building a community's self-defense capacities was always ambivalent. And, because they were ambivalent, the police did not think through the question of whether and how such efforts could actually help them control serious crime.

Problem-solving and community approaches to crime control   In the 1980s, police departments throughout the country began to explore the crime-fighting effectiveness of tactics that build on previous approaches, but seek to extend them by looking behind offenses to the precipitating causes of crimes, building closer relations with the community, and seeking to enhance the self-defense capacities of the communities themselves. These efforts are guided mostly by a theory of what might work and some illustrative examples. The theory is that the effectiveness of existing tactics can be enhanced if the police increase the quantity and quality of their contacts with citizens (both individuals and neighborhood groups), and include in their responses to crime problems thoughtful analyses of the precipitating causes of the offenses. The expectation is that this will both enhance the direct effectiveness of the police department and also enable the police department to leverage the resources of citizen groups and other public agencies to control crime.

Some examples, drawn from recent experiences, suggest the ways in which these new approaches can lead to enhanced crime control.

Enhanced police presence From its inception, patrol has sought to prevent crime through presence, or potential presence, of a conspicuous officer. Patrolling in cars is only one way to communicate police presence, however. Activities such as foot patrol, visiting citizens in their homes, and attending group meetings also increase the awareness of police to which all citizens respond—those intent on crime as well as those not. This presence both deters potential offenders from committing crimes and affords officers the opportunities to note criminal acts in progress.

Example: A youth walking down a street in a small business section of town sees an unlocked automobile with the key in the ignition. He is tempted to steal it. Glancing around, he notes a police officer a short distance away walking down the street. The youth decides not to enter the car for fear of being caught by the officer.

Example: An officer, through crime analysis, becomes aware of a pattern of burglaries in a neighborhood. Increasing her patrol in alleyways, she notes a youth attempting to enter the back window of a residence. She makes an arrest.

Although the success of foot patrol tactics in controlling crime is counter-intuitive to those accustomed to patrol by automobile, confidence in this approach is common in England. There, when an anticrime unit is sent in to deal with a serious crime problem, as often as not it consists of foot patrol. The approach is successful because foot patrol officers have access to areas unavailable to officers in cars: walkways and areas between houses, for example. Unpublished work by Glenn Pierce suggests that some crimes, such as burglary, tend to be patterned within limited geographical and chronological space. If this is true, when combined with what is known about how burglars enter homes and businesses, properly targeted foot patrol might be the strongest potential anticrime tactic to deal with such crimes.

Better surveillance and deterrence of dangerous offenders From the outset, police have sought to control crime through close surveillance of those who have committed crimes in the past. The problem has been to accurately identify those offenders. Police officers who work closely with a neighborhood are in a position to learn who behaves in criminal or delinquent ways within the community. By stationing themselves in particular locations, officers can surveil known troublemakers and forestall criminal behavior.

Example: Police investigation of a rash of robberies committed by juveniles involved house-to-house interviews of the neighborhood. In these interviews, photographs of suspects were shown to residents. While no information about the crimes was produced, the word rapidly spread through the neighborhood that the police were keeping close tabs on specific individuals. The robberies stopped without an arrest.

It is also legally and procedurally possible to consider assigning neighborhood police officers to the surveillance of probationers and parolees. Such surveillance would be more immediate and regular than that now provided by probation or parole officers. Aware that neighborhood police officers had easier access to information about their activities, people who were in the community on a conditional basis might be deterred from committing illegal acts.

Example: Paroled sexual offenders in a conservative state regularly move to a community known for its relatively open values. A plan is worked out between local police and the state correctional agency. Upon parole, all sexual offenders returning to this community are interviewed by the chief of patrol and the neighborhood officer policing the area in which the parolee is to live. An offender known for attacks on teenage girls returns to the community. Regular contacts between the officer and parolee are scheduled to enable the police officer to oversee the parolee's behavior while in the community. The police officer discovers that the parolee is now working in the local fast food restaurant—a workplace which regularly hires teenage girls. The officer, in conjunction with the parole officer, requires that the parolee find a different job, one in which young girls are not always present.

Increased access to information   Community policing emphasizes the development of close communication between citizens and police. This communication helps police gather information for both *preventing* and *solving* crime.

Example: In an area frequented by many street people, a street person approaches a neighborhood police officer to inform him that a stranger from another neighborhood is attempting to recruit assistance to commit a street robbery. The street person describes the newcomer to the police officer. Shortly afterwards while patrolling, the officer notices a person on the street who matches the description. The officer approaches the person, questions him, tells him that he (the officer) is aware of what he is planning, and instructs him to leave the area.

Example: Shortly after leaving her church a woman is mugged on the street. She appears to be seriously injured as a result of being knocked to the ground. Police and medics are called. The neighborhood officer responds on foot. She is approached by several children and their parents. The children were playing in an open space in the public housing project across the street from the church and saw the youth mug the woman. They know the youth and where he lives. Accompanied by a neighborhood entourage, including the parents and children who identified the youth, the officer proceeds to the apartment and makes the arrest.

Familiarity with the social and physical characteristics of their beats also helps neighborhood police officers to understand linkages between various pieces of information gathered from their own observations and from other disparate sources.

Example: Parents have complained to a neighborhood police officer about an increase of drug availability in their neighborhood. Several parents have found drugs in their children's possession. In addition, the officer has noticed many youths congregating around an entrance to a second-story apartment over several stores. The officer contacts the drug unit and informs them of his suspicion that drugs are being sold to children from that apartment. The drug unit arranges an undercover "buy" and then "busts" the dealers.

Work by Pate,[50] Greenwood, Chaiken and Petersilia,[51] Eck,[52] and Skogan and Antunes[53] suggests that use of information gathered by patrol officers is one of the most important ways in which police can improve their ability to apprehend offenders. In 1982, Baltimore County, Maryland, initiated a Citizen Oriented Police Enforcement (COPE) unit, designed to bring the police into closer contact with the citizens and reduce their fears. A 1985 study showed that not only had COPE reduced fear, but also it had apparently produced a 12 percent reduction in the level of reported crime.[54]

Early intervention to prevent the escalation of disorder into crime In a widely read article, Kelling and Wilson argue that there is an important causal link between minor instances of disorder and the occurrence of serious crime.[55] Disorderly behavior—youths congregating, drunks lying down, prostitutes aggressively soliciting— left untended, can escalate into serious crime. The implication is that intervention by police to stop uncivil behavior keeps it from escalating.

Example: Youths panhandle in a subway station. Citizens give money both out of charitable motives and because they are fearful. Youths, emboldened by citizen fear, intimidate and, finally, threaten and mug subway users. Intervention by police to end panhandling by youths reduces threatening and mugging of citizens.

Although this argument has intuitive appeal, little direct empirical evidence exists about exploring its anticrime potential.

Crime prevention activities   An important part of community policing is providing anticrime consultation to citizens, businesses, and other community institutions. The recommendations range from home target hardening (locks, strengthened doors, etc.) to street and building design.

Example: Residents of a neighborhood have been troubled by daytime burglaries. In addition to planning a police response, police consult with homeowners about ways in which they can make their homes more secure from burglars. Suggestions include moving shrubs away from doorways, strengthening locks, securing windows, and taking other burglary prevention precautions.

A 1973 evaluation of Seattle's Community Crime Prevention Program, which used this approach, found a significant reduction in burglaries.[56]

Shoring up community institutions   Institutions of neighborhood social control include families, churches, schools, local businesses, and neighborhood and community organizations. In many communities, the corrosive effects of social disorganization have seriously weakened such organizations. Police, working with such institutions and organizations, can reinforce their normative strength in a community.

Example: Drug dealing is a serious problem in an inner-city neighborhood. Drug dealers not only have dealt drugs freely, but also have intimidated residents to the extent that they are afraid to complain to police. A local church decides that the problem is so serious that an organized effort must be made to attack the problem. Church officials contact the police and ask them to work closely with the neighborhood group. Citizens demonstrate against drug dealing, getting both police protection and great publicity. Citywide and local political leaders, as well as other public and private agencies, become concerned about the problem and develop a concerted effort to reduce drug dealing and intimidation. Sustained street-level enforcement ends drug dealing in that location.

Example: Using up-to-date technology, police are able to identify the patterns of a burglary ring which is moving through a neighborhood. Police contact the local neighborhood anticrime group and inform its members of the patterns so that they can be alert and watch their own and each others' homes.

Example: A woman who lives in public housing has been troubled by attempts of local gangs to recruit her youngest son. Up to now, his older brother has been able to protect him. Now, however, the older brother is going into the service. Approached by the mother, the neighborhood police officer now keeps an eye out for the youngster on the way to and from school as well as on the playground.

Example: A local school is plagued by dropouts who continually hang around the school intimidating both students and teachers. Crime has increased in and around the school. The principal decides to crack down on the problem. The neighborhood police officer becomes involved in the efforts. He teaches a course in youth and the law, increases his surveillance of the grounds, consults with the teachers about handling problems, and invokes other agencies to become involved with the youths who have dropped out of school.

Although promising, it is unclear what impact the strengthening of community institutions has on serious crime. It is an attractive idea, however.

Problem solving   Police have historically viewed calls for service and criminal events as individual incidents. Many such incidents are part of a chronic problem amenable to diagnosis and preventive intervention by either police or other agencies.

Example: Police and citizens note an increase in daytime burglaries in a particular neighborhood. This neighborhood has also been characterized by high rates of truancy. Suspecting that many burglaries are committed by truants, police, citizens, and school officials plan a carefully integrated antitruancy campaign. Daytime burglaries drop.

Problem solving appears to be a promising approach to deter crime. When, in 1985, the Newport News Police Department turned to problem-oriented policing as an approach to dealing with crime, it was successful in dealing with three stubborn crime problems that had beset the community: a series of prostitution-related robberies; a rash of burglaries in a housing project; and larcenies from vehicles parked in downtown areas. In each case, the problem was solved not simply by solving the crimes and arresting offenders, nor by increasing levels of patrol (though both were done), but also by operating on the immediate conditions that were giving rise to the offenses.[57]

These ideas, examples, and results lend plausibility to the notion that problem-solving or community policing can enhance the
crime control capabilities of professional crime fighting. They do
not prove the case, however.

A strategic view of crime fighting   While police executives can
produce increased levels of arrest and local reductions in crime
through the creation of special programs, they are frustrated because they do not know how to produce reductions in citywide levels
of crime. The main reason for this might be that their main force is
not engaged in a serious crime-fighting effort even though it seems
that it is. After all, it would be unreasonable to imagine that any
single small program, typically engaging less than 5 percent of the
force, could have much impact on aggregate levels of crime. The important question is what is the remaining 95 percent of the force
doing? For the most part, the answer is that they are deployed in
patrol cars, responding to calls for service and investigating crimes
after they have occurred. These tactics have only limited effectiveness.

What remains unanswered is the consequence of shifting a
whole department to a radically different style of policing. Moreover, the answer is hard to determine, since the period of transition
would be quite awkward. In the short run, were officers taken from
patrol and detective units to do problem-oriented or community policing, it is almost certain that response times would lengthen—at
least until the problem-solving efforts reduced the demands for service by eliminating the precipitating program that was producing
the calls for service.[58] And even though an increase in response
times does not necessarily indicate a real loss in crime-fighting effectiveness, it would be perceived as such because the public and the
police have learned to equate rapid response to crime calls with
crime control effectiveness.

What is tempting, of course, is to avoid choosing among these
strategies, and to adopt the strengths of these various approaches
while avoiding their weaknesses. This would be reflected in decisions to establish special units to do problem-solving or community
policing within existing organizations whose traditions and main
forces remained committed to reactive patrol and retrospective investigation.

But it may not be this easy. Indeed, experience demonstrates
that it is not. Previous initiatives with team policing or split-force
policing succeeded in building capacities for both styles of policing
within the same department, but tended to foster eventual competition and conflict.[59] The problem-solving and community policing
aspects have usually eventually yielded to administrative demands
to keep response times low, or to officers' desires to avoid the de-

manding engagement with the community. The reason seems to be partly a matter of resources—there has never been enough manpower to maximize performance in both domains at once. But it also seems to be a matter of administrative style and structure. Problem-solving and community policing both require a greater degree of decentralization than does the current policing strategy. They depend more on the initiative of the officers. And they reach out for a close rather than a distant relationship with the community. These are all quite different than the administrative emphases of the current strategy which prescribe centralization, control, and distance from the community.

So while logic and evidence suggest the crime control potential of adding problem-solving and community policing to the concept of rapid response and retrospective investigation, it is hard to add these functions without increasing the resources and significantly changing the administrative style of a police organization. That is hard for a police chief to decide to do without convincing evidence that it would work. The only things that make such a move easy to contemplate are: (1) a deep sense that the current strategy and tactics have reached their limits; (2) the plausibility of the idea that increased effectiveness lies in working on proximate causes and mobilizing communities; and (3) the little bit of evidence we have that the alternative approach works. A few departments, such as Houston, Newport News, Baltimore County, and Philadelphia, have committed themselves to these alternative approaches. If they succeed over the next 3 to 5 years in reducing serious crime as well as in attracting citizen support, then the field will know that it has a better strategy of policing available than is now being used.

1. For descriptions of these alternative strategies, see Robert C. Trojanowicz, "Community Policing vs. 'High Tech' Policing: What's in a Name?" (unpublished paper, Michigan State University, April 1987); Herman Goldstein, *The Urban Police Function* (Cambridge, Mass.: Ballinger Publishing, 1977); John Eck and William Spelman, "Solving Problems: Problem-Oriented Policing in Newport News" (Washington, D.C.: Police Executive Research Forum, January 1987).

2. George L. Kelling and Mark H. Moore, "From Political to Reform to Community: The Evolving Strategy of Police" (Program in Criminal Justice Policy and Management, John F. Kennedy School of Government, Harvard University, Cambridge, 1987), Working Paper #87-05-08.

3. President's Commission on Law Enforcement and Administration of Justice, *Task Force Report: Science and Technology* (Washington, D.C.: U.S. Government Printing Office, 1967). Jan M. Chaiken and Warren Walker, *Patrol Car Allocation Model* (Santa Monica: The Rand Corporation, 1985). Richard C. Larson, *Police Deployment from Urban Public Safety Systems*, Vol. I (Lexington, Mass.: Lexington Books, 1978). David M. Kennedy, "Patrol Allocation in Portland, OR, Part A: PCAM in the Bureau," Case #C95-88-818.0

and "Patrol Allocation in Portland, OR, Part B: PCAM in the City," Case #C95-88-819.0 (Cambridge: Case Program, John F. Kennedy School of Government, 1988).

4. J. Thomas McEwen, Edward F. Connors III, and Marcia Cohen, *Evaluation of the Differential Police Response Field Test* (Washington, D.C.: U.S. Government Printing Office, 1986). Richard P. Grassie and John A. Hollister, *Integrated Criminal Apprehension Program: A Preliminary Guideline Manual for Patrol Operations Analysis* (Washington, D.C.: LEAA, U.S. Department of Justice, 1977).

5. James Q. Wilson, "The Police and Crime," in *Thinking About Crime* (New York: Vintage Books, 1975), Chapter 4, Larson, *Police Deployment from Urban Public Safety Systems.*

6. Orlando W. Wilson, *The Distribution of the Police Patrol Force* (Chicago: Public Administration Service, 1941).

7. Alfred Blumstein et al., *Deterrence and Incapacitation: Estimating the Effects of Criminal Sanctions on the Crime Rate* (Washington, D.C.: National Academy of Sciences, 1978).

8. Ibid.

9. Mark H. Moore, *Buy and Bust: The Effective Regulation of an Illicit Market in Heroin* (Lexington, Mass.: Lexington Books, 1977). Peter K. Manning, *The Narc's Game: Organizational and Informational Limits on Drug Law Enforcement* (Cambridge: MIT Press, 1980). Mark H. Moore, "Invisible Offenses: A Challenge to Minimally Intrusive Law Enforcement," in Gerald M. Caplan, ed., *Abscam Ethics* (Washington, D.C.: Police Foundation, 1983). Gary Marx, "Who Really Gets Stung? Some Issues Raised by the New Police Undercover Work," in Caplan, *Abscam Ethics.*

10. George L. Kelling, "Juveniles and Police: The End of the Nightstick," in Francis X. Hartman, ed., *From Children to Citizens*, Vol. 2: *The Role of the Juvenile Court* (New York:

Springer-Verlag, 1987).

11. The exception is Marvin Wolfgang's work devoted to measuring crime seriousness as perceived by citizens. See Marvin E. Wolfgang and Thorsten Sellin, *The Measurement of Crime Seriousness* (New York: Wiley Publishing, 1964). See also Mark H. Moore et al., *Dangerous Offenders: The Elusive Target of Justice* (Cambridge: Harvard University Press, 1984), Chapter 2.

12. Bureau of Justice Statistics, *The Severity of Crime* (Washington, D.C.: U.S. Department of Justice, January 1984), p. 5.

13. Susan Estrich, *Real Rape* (Cambridge: Harvard University Press, 1987).

14. Bureau of Justice Statistics, *The Severity of Crime.*

15. Ibid.

16. For a view of crime as a dispute rather than an attack, see Donald Black, *The Manners and Customs of the Police* (New York: Academic Press, 1980), Chapter 5. For important empirical evidence, see Vera Institute of Justice, *Felony Arrests: Their Prosecution and Disposition in the New York City Courts* (New York, 1981).

17. Bureau of Justice Statistics, "Households Touched by Crime 1986," *BJS Bulletin* (Washington, D.C.: U.S. Department of Justice, June 1987).

18. Bureau of Justice Statistics, *Report to the Nation on Crime and Justice* (Washington, D.C.: U.S. Department of Justice, 1983).

19. Patrick W. O'Carroll and James A. Mercy, "Patterns and Recent Trends in Black Homicide," in Darnell F. Hawkins, ed., *Homicide among Black Americans* (Lanham, Md.: University Press of America, 1986).

20. Bureau of Justice Statistics, "Households Touched by Crime."

21. James Q. Wilson, "Criminologists," in *Thinking about Crime* (New York: Vintage Books, 1975), Chapter 3.

22. For a discussion of this concept and its importance to police strategies, see Moore et al., *Dangerous Offend-*

ers, Chapter 7.

23. Alfred Blumstein et al., *Criminal Careers and Career Criminals*, Vol. 1 (Washington, D.C.: National Academy Press, 1986).

24. Jan Chaiken and Marcia Chaiken, *Varieties of Criminal Behavior* (Santa Monica, Calif.: The Rand Corporation, August 1982).

25. Peter W. Greenwood and Sue Turner, *Selective Incapacitation, Revisited for the National Institute of Justice* (Santa Monica, Calif.: The Rand Corporation, 1987).

26. Moore et al., *Dangerous Offenders.*

27. Glenn Pierce et al., "Evaluation of an Experiment in Proactive Police Intervention in the Field of Domestic Violence Using Repeat Call Analysis" (Boston, Mass.: The Boston Fenway Program, Inc., May 13, 1987).

28. Lawrence W. Sherman, "Repeat Calls to Police in Minneapolis" (College Park, Md.: University of Maryland, 1987).

29. This example of youth transportation comes from Christine Nixon's experience in New South Wales, Australia. For other examples, see John Eck and William Spelman, "Solving Problems: Problem-Oriented Policing."

30. Mark H. Moore, "Controlling Criminogenic Commodities: Drugs, Guns, and Alcohol," in James Q. Wilson, ed., *Crime and Public Policy* (San Francisco: Institute for Contemporary Studies Press, 1983).

31. Eric Wish, "Drug Use Forecasting System" (unpublished working paper at the National Institute of Justice, Washington, D.C., January 1988).

32. Ibid.

33. Marvin E. Wolfgang, *Patterns in Criminal Homicide* (Montclair, N.J.: Patterson Smith Publishing, 1975). James Collins, *Alcohol Use and Criminal Behavior: An Executive Summary* (Washington, D.C.: U.S. Department of Justice, 1981).

34. Mark H. Moore, "Drugs and Crime: A Policy Analytic Approach," Appendix to Report of the Panel on Drug Use and Criminal Behavior, *Drug Use and Crime* (Washington, D.C.: National Institute on Drug Abuse and Research Triangle Institute, 1976).

35. David Levinson, "Alcohol Use and Aggression in American Subcultures," in Robin Room and Gary Collins, eds., *Alcohol and Disinhibition: Nature and Meaning of the Link* (Washington, D.C.: U.S. Department of Health and Human Services, 1983).

36. Moore, "Controlling Criminogenic Commodities."

37. Wolfgang, *Patterns in Criminal Homicide.*

38. M. Douglas Anglin and Yih-Ing Hser, "Treatment of Drug Abuse," manuscript to be published in Michael Tonry and James Q. Wilson, eds., *Drugs and Crime*, a special volume of *Crime and Justice: A Review of Research* (Chicago: University of Chicago Press, forthcoming).

39. Sherman, "Repeat Calls to Police in Minneapolis."

40. George L. Kelling, *Kansas City Preventive Patrol Experiment: A Summary Report* (Washington, D.C.: Police Foundation, 1974).

41. *Response Time Analysis* (Kansas City, Mo.: Kansas City Police Department, 1977).

42. Peter W. Greenwood, Jan M. Chaiken, and Joan Petersilia, *The Criminal Investigation Process* (Lexington, Mass.: D.C. Heath, 1977). John Eck, *Managing Case Assignments: Burglary Investigation Decision Model Replication* (Washington, D.C.: Police Executive Research Forum, 1979).

43. Moore, "Invisible Offenses."

44. Antony Pate, Robert Bowers, and Ron Parks, *Three Approaches to Criminal Apprehension in Kansas City: An Evaluation Report* (Washington, D.C.: Police Foundation, 1976).

45. Jerome E. McElroy, Colleen Cosgrove, and Michael Farrell, *Felony Case Preparation: Quality Counts*, Interim Report of the New York City Police Department Felony

Case Preparation Project (New York: Vera Institute of Justice, 1981).

46. Grassie and Hollister, *Integrated Criminal Apprehension Program.*
47. Moore et al., *Dangerous Offenders,* Chapter 7.
48. Marx, "Who Really Gets Stung?"
49. Wesley G. Skogan and George E. Antunes, "Information, Apprehension, and Deterrence: Exploring the Limits of Police Productivity," *Journal of Criminal Justice,* 1979, No. 7, pp. 217-242.
50. Pate et al., *Three Approaches to Criminal Apprehension.*
51. Greenwood et al., *The Criminal Investigative Process.*
52. Eck, *Managing Case Assignments.*
53. Skogan and Antunes, "Information, Apprehension, and Deterrence."
54. Philip B. Taft, Jr., "Fighting Fear: The Baltimore County COPE Project" (Washington, D.C.: Police Executive Research Forum, February 1986), p. 20.
55. James Q. Wilson and George L. Kelling, "Broken Windows," *Atlantic Monthly,* March 1982, pp. 29-38.

56. Betsy Lindsay and Daniel McGillis, "Citywide Community Crime Prevention: An Assessment of the Seattle Program," in Dennis P. Rosenbaum, ed., *Community Crime Prevention: Does It Work?* (Beverly Hills, Calif.: Sage Publications, 1986).
57. Eck and Spelman, "Solving Problems: Problem-Oriented Policing."
58. Calls for service declined in Flint, Michigan, after foot patrol was established and officers were handling less serious complaints informally. Robert Trojanowicz, *An Evaluation of the Neighborhood Foot Patrol Program in Flint, Michigan* (East Lansing: Michigan State University, 1982), pp. 29-30.
59. George L. Kelling and Mary Ann Wycoff, *The Dallas Experience: Human Resource Development* (Washington, D.C.: Police Foundation, 1978). James Tien et al., *An Alternative Approach in Police Patrol: The Wilmington Split-Force Experiment* (Cambridge, Mass.: Public Systems Evaluation Inc., 1977).

The Police and Delivery of Local Government Services: A Problem-Oriented Approach

William Spelman and John E. Eck

Drug dealers have taken over a park. Neighborhood residents, afraid to use the park, feel helpless. Foot patrols and drug raids fail to roust the dealers.

A city is hit with a rash of convenience store robberies. Stakeouts, fast response to robbery calls, and enhanced investigations lead to some arrests—but do not solve the robbery problem.

Disorderly kids invade a peaceful residential neighborhood. Although they have committed no serious crimes, they are noisy and unpredictable; some acts of vandalism have been reported. The kids are black and the residents white—and the police fear a racial incident.

Problems like these plague cities everywhere. Social incivilities, drug dealing and abuse, and violent crime hurt more than the immediate victims: they create fears among the rest of us. We wonder who will be next but feel incapable of taking action.

Until recently, there had been little the criminal justice system could do to help. Police continued to respond to calls for service and attempted (usually without success) to arrest and punish the most serious criminals. Sometimes they tried to organize a neighborhood watch. But research conducted in the 1970s and early 1980s showed repeatedly that these strategies had only limited effectiveness.

Since the mid-1980s, some innovative police departments have begun to test new approaches to these problems. These "problem-oriented" approaches differ from the traditional methods in several ways:

1. Police actively seek ways to prevent crime and better the

quality of neighborhood life, rather than simply react to calls for service and reported crimes.
2. Police recognize that standardized responses often are inadequate. Crime and disorder problems arise from a variety of conditions, and thorough analysis is needed before police can tailor effective responses to these conditions.
3. The size and nature of many crime and disorder problems depend upon factors beyond the control of any single public or private agency. If these problems are to be solved, they must be attacked by many people, on many different fronts. That is, the police, the public, and other agencies must "co-produce" neighborhood security.

Recent research shows that when police adopt a proactive stance, analyze local conditions, and recognize the value of co-production in framing and implementing a response, they can reduce crime and fear of crime. The problem-oriented approach has profound implications for the management and operation of police agencies and for the relationship between the police and the communities they serve.

The problem: The incident-driven approach

Problem-oriented policing is the culmination of more than two decades of research into the nature of crime and the effectiveness of police response. Many strands of research led to the new approach, but three basic findings were particularly important:

1. Additional police resources, if applied in response to individual incidents of crime and disorder, will be ineffective in controlling crime.
2. Few incidents are isolated; most are symptoms of some recurring, underlying problem. Problem analysis can help police develop effective, proactive tactics.
3. Crime problems are integrally linked to other urban problems, and so the most effective responses require coordinating the activities of private citizens, the business sector, and government agencies outside the criminal justice system.

In short, "incident-driven policing," the prevailing method of delivering police services, consistently treats symptoms, not diseases. By working with others to identify, analyze, and treat diseases, police can make headway against crime and disorder.

Adding police resources will be ineffective   Most police work is reactive—a response to crimes and disorders reported by the public. And current, reactive tactics may be effective at controlling crime, to a point. For example, by maintaining some threat of apprehension and punishment, current police actions may deter many would-be offenders.[1]

Nevertheless, twenty years of research into police operations suggest that the marginal value of additional police resources, if applied in the traditional, reactive ways, will be very small.[2] For example, interception patrol tactics probably will not deter offenders unless the patrol force can be increased dramatically—perhaps by a factor of thirty or more.[3] Only ten percent of crimes are reported to the police within five minutes of occurrence; thus, for the vast majority of crimes,[4] even the fastest police response will not generally result in apprehension of a suspect. And clearance rates are low, because detectives rarely have many leads to work with; even if the number of detectives could be doubled or tripled, it would have virtually no effect on the number of successful clearances.[5]

Split force, investigative case screening, differential response to calls, and similar deployment methods succeeded in shifting scarce resources to those incidents where they were most needed.[6] These schemes, often directed by crime analysis, made police operations more efficient and freed up resources for other activities. But they did not make operations more effective.

Crime analysis can lead to more effective tactics   Three elements must be present before a crime will be committed: Someone must be motivated to commit the crime; a suitable target must be present; and the target must be (relatively) unguarded, providing the offender with an opportunity to commit the crime.[7] These elements are more likely to be present at some times and places than at others, forming crime patterns and recurring crime problems. Since all three elements must generally be present before a crime will be committed, the problem can be solved by removing just one of the elements. By identifying the elements that are easiest to remove and working to remove them, police can make crime prevention tactics both more efficient and more effective.

The most obvious crime patterns are spatial. Since the 1930s, researchers have shown that crime types and offender methods of operation—not to mention gross crime rates—differed substantially among neighborhoods.[8]

One reason for these differences is that there are more unguarded opportunities in some neighborhoods than in others. For example, neighborhoods with diverse land uses, single-family houses and garden apartment buildings, and intense street lighting provide criminals with fewer opportunities and incur lower crime rates.[9] Social characteristics such as residential stability, homogeneity of lifestyle, and family orientation empower residents of a neighborhood to deal with miscreants without calling the police.[10]

Another reason crime rates differ among neighborhoods is that some areas are home to more offenders and victims than others. Adolescents and the poor commit property crimes at higher rates than the rest of the population. Since poor youths have few sources of transportation out of their neighborhoods, it is not surprising that burglary and robbery rates are highest in neighborhoods where many poor youths live. Some neighborhoods attract more than their share of offenders because open-air drug markets or bars that cater to the especially rowdy or criminal are located there. Furthermore, potential victims who have the money to do so can make themselves unattractive or even unavailable to offenders by keeping valuables in safe-deposit boxes or safes, garaging their cars, buying houses with sturdy locks and alarms, or moving to the suburbs.

Thus, neighborhood crime patterns differ in predictable ways for comprehensible reasons. The implications for crime prevention policies are obvious: if our aim is to reduce the crime rate in a given neighborhood, clearly it is important to know what kinds of crimes are committed there and what might be done to reduce the number of available offenders or victims or else to increase the number of willing and able guardians. Since neighborhoods differ, officers assigned to an area must study the social and physical conditions there before developing and implementing prevention strategies.

These strategies are given a focus by one regularity that seems to hold for crime problems in all neighborhoods: crime is concentrated. A relatively small number of frequent offenders commit most of the serious crimes.[11] A few particularly vulnerable people run risks of victimization that are much higher than average.[12] And a disproportionate share of crimes are committed at a few particularly dangerous locations.[13] Research suggests that there are usually good reasons why these offenders, victims, and locations account for so many crimes. If something can be done about these "ravenous wolves," "sitting ducks," and "dens of iniquity," the crime problem can, in theory, be reduced dramatically.

Current police policies systematically overlook the most crime-prone people and places. For example, until recently, police gave little attention to cases of family violence—even though abused family members suffer particularly high risks of being abused again.[14] If repeat calls to a single location are made at different times of the day, they will be distributed over several shifts, and therefore even the beat officers may not recognize the continuing nature of the problem. The most frequent offenders are also the most successful at evading arrest.[15]

These concentrations of crimes among victims, locations, and offenders are important handles for proactive crime prevention activity. They are the "problems" that are the focus of problem-oriented policing. Government and private agencies have mounted a wide variety of programs aimed at preventing these most predictable of crimes. For example, police, prosecutors, judges, and parole boards have adopted programs and policies aimed at deterrence and incapacitation of frequent, serious offenders.[16] Many recent crime prevention efforts have focused on especially vulnerable people, such as abused spouses, the elderly, and the mentally disabled. Through directed patrols[17] and environmental and situational crime prevention,[18] police and other agencies have begun to deal with crime-prone locations, as well.

The nature of these concentrations is different for every problem, however, so standardized responses will not generally succeed. Previous experience can be a guide, but police must study and create a somewhat different response for each problem they take on.

Neighborhood problems are not easily separable   It may be helpful to know whether a given crime or disorder problem results from frequent offenders, high-risk victims, vulnerable locations, or some combination of the three. But this knowledge is often insufficient to allow the police to identify a workable solution. To solve many problems, the police need the help of outside agencies, the business sector, or the public. Often this help is needed because the police lack the authority to remove the offending conditions. If a rowdy bar produces many assaults, it can be closed down—by the state alcoholic beverage control board. If a blind corner produces many auto accidents, a stoplight can be installed—by the traffic department. If a woman is continually beaten by her husband, she can move out—but the police cannot force her to do so.

Perhaps a more important reason is that recurring problems have many parts, and no single agency is responsible for all of them. A run-down apartment complex may look like a serious burglary problem to the police. But the fire department sees a high risk of fire in vacant apartments. The housing department sees code violations, and the health department sees an abundance of trash and rats. The bank sees a bad risk and refuses to loan the apartment owner the money needed to renovate the vacant apartments that have been taken over by the drug addicts who commit the burglaries. The residents, beset on all sides, see no hope—they cannot afford cleaner and safer housing.

Clearly, no single agency will be able to solve this problem, because the various parts feed off one another. On the other hand, if all the parts can be addressed at the same time, it is possible that the conditions can be removed and the problem solved. This would require the cooperation of the police, fire, housing, and health departments; the bank; and the apartment owner. It might also require the help of the residents, to ensure that the appropriate agencies are notified should the problem start to return.

There is evidence that citizens, in particular, co-produce crime control with public agencies. In addition to cooperating with the police and pressuring public and private agencies to deliver the goods and services the neighborhood needs, citizens sometimes intervene directly in disorderly or criminal incidents. Although some experts maintain that these informal interventions are the most important determinants of a neighborhood's crime rate, they are difficult to maintain in high-crime areas. The physical design of urban neighborhoods—of public housing, in particular—discourages surveillance and intervention by neighbors.[19] Often the residents of these poor neighborhoods have little in common, do not expect to stay long, have little reason to care for one another, and do not even recognize one another. These characteristics make it hard for neighbors to control the minor disorders that may contribute to crime. When many families are headed by single parents who must work, parents may not even be able to control their own children.[20] On the other hand, the physical and social environment of high-crime neighborhoods can be improved by governments and businesses; the improvements, in turn, increase the prospects for intervention and co-production.

All these findings suggest that crime prevention strategies are incomplete and possibly ineffective unless they recognize the close links among crime, the physical environment, neighborhood culture, and other factors. In general, these links require that the public and outside agencies work with the police to eliminate or ameliorate the conditions that cause the problem.

Police can be more effective if they reduce their reliance on traditional methods and rely instead on tailor-made responses to specific problems, responses that coordinate the activities of people and agencies both inside and outside the criminal justice system. How would such a police department work? How would it be structured? How well would it control crime and disorder? The experiences of innovative departments in using a problem-oriented approach suggest some intriguing answers.

A solution: Problem-oriented policing

Problem-oriented policing is a new approach to police work that changes the basic nature of police service. Unlike incident-driven policing, it is proactive rather than reactive; it emphasizes careful analysis and tailor-made responses rather than lockstep application of standard operating procedures. Perhaps most important, problem-oriented policing requires officers to work with the community, other public agencies, and others to identify and analyze problems and to develop and implement solutions.

Designing problem-oriented policing The heart of problem-oriented policing is systematic thinking. Problem solving has been conducted in different ways in different departments. The most methodical approach has been adopted in Newport News, Virginia.

Darrel Stephens, then Newport News police chief, wanted his agency's problem-solving system to be based on three principles. First, officers of all ranks, from all units, should be able to use the procedures as part of their daily routine. Second, the system must encourage officers to collect information from a broad range of sources and not limit themselves to conventional police data. Finally, the system should encourage co-production solutions not limited to the criminal justice process.

After several months of work, a departmental task force developed a problem-solving process that fit these criteria. It consisted of four parts:

1. *Scanning.* Officers are expected to look for possible problems as part of their daily routine.
2. *Analysis.* Officers then collect information about the problem. They rely on a problem analysis guide, developed by the task force, which directs officers to examine offenders, victims, the social and physical environment, and previous responses to the problem. The goal is to understand the scope, nature, and causes of the problem.
3. *Response.* The knowledge gained in the analysis stage is then used to develop and implement solutions. Officers seek the assistance of other police units, other public and private organizations, and anyone else who can help.
4. *Assessment.* Finally, officers evaluate the effectiveness of their responses. They may use the results to revise a response, collect more data, or even to redefine the problem.

Newport News's systematic process has since been adopted by other agencies interested in problem solving, including San Diego, Tulsa, and New York City. Similar approaches have been adopted, although less explicitly, by most police agencies that have experimented with problem-oriented policing.

Problem-solving in practice Since the early 1980s, police agencies have applied a problem-oriented approach to a wide variety of problems. To illustrate the breadth of problems and solutions that are possible, we describe three case studies.[21] First, we examine two serious and complex problems—one affecting a residential neighborhood, the other affecting an entire city—that succumbed to careful analysis and comprehensive responses. Then we look at another, apparently difficult, neighborhood problem that was solved in only a few hours through careful observation and a little thought.

New York retirees sting drug dealers   Sunset Park in Brooklyn is a neighborhood of row houses and small businesses peopled by a mix of working- and middle-class Irish, Italians, Puerto Ricans, and blacks. Sunset Park is clean, and many streets are lined with trees. The district is dotted with vestpocket parks containing such amenities as handball and basketball courts for the vigorous, sandboxes and swings for the young, and sunny benches for the relaxed.

Despite these amenities, for years the neighborhood park had lured only drug users looking for a quick score. Respectable residents avoided the park, fearing confrontations with the drug traffickers. The New York Police Department tried to respond to the problem, directing its officers to patrol the park and issue loitering citations to apparent dealers. This dispersed the dealers and users—until the patrol car had turned the corner and disappeared from view. Then business returned to normal. Not surprisingly, the problem persisted.

In May 1986, Officer Vinny Esposito was assigned to the 49th Street beat, which included Sunset Park. As one of the first members of New York's innovative Community Patrol Officer Program (CPOP), Esposito was expected to do more than just handle individual incidents on his beat. His job was to identify and solve recurring problems. The drug-ridden 49th Street park clearly fit the bill, and Esposito went to work.

At first, Esposito used the old tactics. He spent as much time in the park as he could, dispersing dealers and making arrests whenever possible. Unfortunately, his beat was large, and the time he could spend in the park was limited. Worse yet, every arrest took him away from the park for an hour or more—and whenever he left, the junkies returned. Weeks passed with no apparent effect on the drug trade. Esposito considered the problem further and decided to take a different tack.

He began by recognizing that loitering citations and even drug arrests were at worst minor inconveniences to the dealers and users, since few arrests led to jail or prison terms. On the other hand, Esposito reasoned, the threat of losing hundreds or thousands of dollars worth of drugs could be a serious deterrent. Dealers, recognizing their vulnerability in the event of a police field stop, typically hid their stashes in the park. So Esposito could seize the dope if he knew where it was hidden—but that required the assistance of local residents.

Esposito held meetings of the tenants in the apartment buildings that overlooked the park. Many tenants were elderly and spent most of their days at home. Esposito asked them to watch the dealers from their windows and report to the local precinct station the location of any drug stashes they saw. Reassured that their tips would remain completely anonymous, the frustrated tenants readily agreed to help.

Calls began coming in. A CPOP officer at the precinct station would take down the information and radio the location of the stash to Officer Esposito, who would then confiscate the drugs and take them to the station. Twenty minutes after the tip had been phoned in, Esposito was back on the beat and a dealer was a little bit poorer.

This new strategy had several effects. Some dealers found themselves having to explain to unsympathetic suppliers where their goods had gone. Others began keeping their stashes on their person, making them more vulnerable to arrest. Others simply quit the park. Within one month all the dealers had gotten the message—and the park was free of drugs.

Today the park is a different place. Children play on the swings; youths play basketball. Many of the older residents who once sat at home phoning in anonymous tips now spend their days sunning themselves on the benches of "their" park. They show no signs of giving it back to the dealers.

As in the Sunset Park case, many persistent problems affect residents of small neighborhoods. As Officer Esposito's actions illustrate, these problems can often be solved with the help of neighborhood residents. Neighborhood problem-solving, sometimes called "community policing," is an important part of the problem-oriented approach. But other persistent problems, not restricted to small localities and affecting residents throughout the city, require citywide changes in policies and practices. Sometimes there is a citywide "community of interest" that can be relied on to assist the police in solving the problem, in much the same way that the elderly residents of Sunset Park helped clear the drug dealers out of their vestpocket park. Merchant associations, chain retail stores, and citywide community groups may all be of assistance. Even when these communities are uncooperative, however, the police may still be able to solve the problem, as is illustrated in the experience of Gainesville, Florida.

Gainesville puts the brakes on convenience store crime When the university town of Gainesville, Florida, was hit with a rash of convenience store robberies in the spring of 1985, the police recognized that they were dealing with more than just a series of unrelated incidents. The department's crime analysts had expected to find that one or two repeat offenders were responsible for the robberies, but suspect descriptions provided by the victims proved that many different offenders were responsible. Word had apparently gotten around that convenience stores were an easy target. Police Chief Wayland Clifton, Jr., wondered why and detailed several members of his department to find out.

Gainesville police officers compared the stores that had been robbed to stores that had not. Their conclusions were revealing. Many of the stores that had been robbed had posted large advertisements in their front windows, blocking the view from the street. Often, the checkout stand could not be seen by a passing car or pedestrian. Many stores failed to light their parking lots, further limiting visibility. Others kept large sums of money in the cash register, and some provided only one inexperienced employee during the late night hours. The stores that had not been robbed tended to provide better visibility, limit the amount of cash in the register, and train their employees in crime prevention techniques. Thus, the criminals seemed to be focusing on the most lucrative and vulnerable targets.

The police department presented these findings to an association of local merchants that had been established to develop a response to the problem. The police asked for a commitment to change the conditions that made robberies easy to commit. They were disappointed: the merchants felt that the solution lay in more frequent police patrols and refused to agree to voluntary crime prevention standards. In effect, the merchants argued that the costs of convenience store crime prevention should be borne by the public as a whole rather than by the stores themselves.

Chief Clifton had read the research and knew that he could not stop the robberies with police presence unless he assigned his officers to stand guard at every convenience store in the city. Instead, he directed his officers to search for another way of mandating crime prevention measures. Their research revealed that the cities of Akron, Ohio, and Coral Gables, Florida, had passed ordinances requiring merchants to take certain crime prevention measures and that these ordinances had reduced the incidence of robbery. Clifton and his officers began drafting such an ordinance for Gainesville.

By the summer of 1986, the police were ready to present their findings to the city commission. The department's ordinance would require convenience stores to remove window advertising, place cash registers in full view of the street, install security cameras and outside lighting, and limit the amount of cash available in the register. Most important, it would require two or more employees trained in crime prevention techniques to work late at night. In July the city commission overruled the objections of the convenience store owners and passed the ordinance.

The store owners fought the ordinance in court, arguing that the crime prevention measures would be costly and ineffective. But the judge found the police department's research to be persuasive. The store owners' injunction was denied, and the ordinance took effect on schedule.

In the first year after adoption, the new ordinance had encouraging results: convenience store robberies were down by 65 percent overall and by 75 percent at night. Best of all, the robbery rate was reduced far below its pre-1985 levels. Convenience stores continue to do a land-office business in Gainesville, and many store owners now admit—a bit grudgingly—that the police department's citywide approach has solved a difficult problem.

Persistent problems such as the convenience store robberies in Gainesville are natural targets of problem-solving. It is easy to see how time-consuming research and complex crime prevention measures can be worth the effort if they will help to remove a longstanding problem. But many crime and disorder problems are temporary and nagging rather than persistent and severe; they do not merit lengthy analysis and complicated responses. Still, thinking systematically about even a minor problem can often reveal a quick solution that is easy to implement, as is illustrated in the following case.

Newport News skates out of trouble   The quiet nights of a middle-class Newport News neighborhood were spoiled when groups of rowdy teenagers began to frequent the area on Fridays and Saturdays. There had been no violence, and the kids' primary offenses were loud music, horseplay, and occasional vandalism. But residents felt the teenagers were unpredictable, particularly since they came from the city's mostly black southeast side, several miles away. The neighborhood became a regular stop for officers working the evening shift.

Sergeant Jim Hogan recognized that responding to these calls took time but accomplished little except to irritate everyone involved. One Friday night he asked the beat officer, Paul Summerfield, to look into the problem and develop a better solution.

Summerfield suspected that the source of the problem might be a roller skating rink. The rink had been trying to increase business by offering reduced rates and transportation on Friday and Saturday nights. As he drove north toward the rink later that night, Summerfield saw several large groups of youths walking south. Other kids were still hanging around the rink, which had closed shortly before. Summerfield talked to several of them and found that they were waiting for a bus. The other kids, he was told, had become impatient and had begun the three-mile walk home. Then Summerfield talked to the rink owner. The owner had leased the bus to pick up and drop off kids who lived far from the rink. But there were always more kids needing rides at the end of the night than the bus had picked up earlier.

When he returned to the skating rink early the next evening, Officer Summerfield saw fifty or so youngsters get out of the bus rented by the skating rink. But he saw others get out of the public transit buses, which stopped running at midnight. And he saw parents drop their kids off and then turn around and go home. Clearly the rink's bus would be unable to take home all the kids who would be there at closing time. Summerfield consulted Sergeant Hogan. They agreed that the skating rink owner should be asked to bus the kids home. Summerfield returned to the rink on Monday and spoke with the owner. When informed of the size of the problem he had unwittingly created, the owner agreed to lease more buses. By the next weekend the buses were in use, and Summerfield and Hogan saw no kids walking home.

Elapsed time from problem identification to problem solution: one week. Resources used: about four hours of an officer's time. Results: fewer calls, happier kids, satisfied homeowners.

Institutionalizing problem-oriented policing   Problem-oriented policing is an approach—not a program, a technique, or a procedure. Problem-solving procedures and analysis guides can be helpful, but only if they encourage clear-headed analysis of problems and an uninhibited search for solutions. Moreover, there are any number of ways to implement the approach. The New York Police Department established a special unit to focus on neighborhood problems full time; in Newport News, all officers are obliged to spend some of their time identifying and working on problems. There is a place for problem solving in any agency's standard operating procedures. In the long run it is likely that the problem-oriented approach will have a dramatic impact on the management structure of American policing and on the relationship of the police to other city agencies and to the public.

Changes in management structure   As the case studies suggest, crime and disorder problems are fundamentally local and specialized in nature. As a result, they are best analyzed and responded to on a case-by-case basis by the line officers and detectives assigned to the neighborhood or crime type. This will require changes in the centralized, control-oriented organizational structure and management style of most police agencies. Command staff and midlevel managers can structure problem-solving efforts by creating standard operating procedures, such as the problem-solving process created in Newport News, and they can encourage effective and innovative efforts by rewarding the officers who undertake them. But they cannot make the many individual decisions that are required to identify, analyze, and solve problems.

Inevitably, the changes in structure and style will affect line supervisors—sergeants—the most. Problem solving puts a dual burden on supervisors. On the one hand, they must make many of the tough operational decisions—setting priorities among different problems, facilitating communication and cooperation with other divisions of the police department and outside agencies, and making sure their officers solve the problems they are assigned. On the other hand, sergeants must also provide leadership, encouraging creative analysis and response. As the sergeant's role shifts from taskmaster to team leader, police agencies must take greater care in selecting, training, and rewarding their line supervisors.

As the structure and style of police agencies change, the agencies must also shift their focus from internal management problems to the external problems of the public. When a few routine procedures such as preventive patrol, rapid response, and follow-up investigations formed the bulk of an agency's activity, the manager's job was mostly to remove barriers to efficient execution of these routines. Good managers streamlined administrative procedures and reduced paperwork, implemented new resource deployment schemes, and structured officer discretion.[22] They did not need to emphasize crime and disorder reduction, since crimes and disorders would presumably take care of themselves if the routines were implemented properly.

On the other hand, problem-solving activities are inherently nonroutine; it is far more important to choose the correct response from among many—to "do the right thing"—than it is to "do things right." Thus, managers must shift their focus from internal efficiency measures to external effectiveness measures. Instead of citywide clearance and arrest rates, police must emphasize neighborhood crime rates; instead of counting the number of tickets written by all officers, they must count the number of auto accidents on particular stretches of road. Police must recognize that problem-specific crime rates, accident rates, and the like are partly within their control. While no agency can be held accountable for citywide crime and accident rates, police managers and officers must accept partial responsibility for conditions in their areas.

Changes in police role Of course, crime, disorder, and other evils are only partly the responsibility of the police. As the three case studies illustrate, police agencies cannot solve these problems by themselves; they need help from other public service agencies, the business community, and the public. The need to obtain cooperation and assistance from these co-producers of public safety requires that the role of the police agency change.

One fundamental change will be in the autonomy of the police relative to other public service agencies. Urban bureaucracies are currently structured along functional lines—public works maintains roads and sewers, code enforcement ensures that building codes are met, and so on. But if urban problems are interrelated and concentrated, as the research and case studies presented suggest, then these functional distinctions begin to blur. The activities of each public service department affect (and perhaps worsen) the problems of all other departments; therefore, at a minimum, they must communicate to one another what they are doing about a problem and why. A more ambitious and effective strategy would be for them to develop and implement a common response. In the short run, each agency gives up some of its "turf"; in the long run, each agency saves itself a lot of work.

The turf problems resulting from absence of cooperative action are not trivial. One classic example is the "rat problem":

If a rat is found in an apartment, it is a housing inspection responsibility; if it runs into a restaurant, the health department has jurisdiction; if it goes outside and dies in an alley, public works takes over.[23]

Clearly, agencies unwilling to sacrifice any of their autonomy can find endless opportunities to pass the buck.

In the short run, problem-oriented police agencies have found that line personnel in other agencies can be "hidden allies," bending procedures to get the job done. For example, one police agency attempted to solve a recurring traffic accident problem by trying to convince the traffic engineer to install a stop sign at the blind corner. The engineer refused to comply until he had conducted his own study; unfortunately, many similar problems were already awaiting study, so the engineer would not be able to consider the corner for several months. Then a police officer discovered that the public works personnel who actually installed the signs could replace a missing or deteriorated sign within a few days and that the roadworkers would be happy to install the "missing" stop sign. The work order was placed, and the sign was installed within a week. Now police officers in this jurisdiction regularly bypass the traffic engineer and deal directly with public works officials.

Hidden allies may help get the job done; but in the long run, turf difficulties are best surmounted when top managers—city managers and department heads—recognize the value of a cooperative, problem-oriented approach and urge their managers and line personnel to comply. This puts the onus on problem-oriented police administrators to educate and lobby their colleagues, running interference for their officers. As will be described, such an educational effort may ultimately result in substantial changes in the city bureaucracy.

Problem-oriented policing also requires that police take on a different role with regard to the public they serve. At present, police ask little more of citizens than that they report crimes, be good witnesses, and stand aside to let the professionals do their job. As with public service agencies, however, problem solving requires that the police and the public communicate and cooperate more frequently, on a wider variety of issues. In particular, problem-oriented police agencies recognize that citizens often know their problems more intimately than the police do and that sometimes citizens know better what must be done.

This raises many difficult questions. Just as different public service agencies see different aspects of a problem, so do different groups of citizens. If there is no consensus among the community of interest as to the nature of the problem, but public cooperation is necessary to solve it, the police must play a role in forging this consensus. Few police agencies, however, are well equipped for such essentially political activities.

The dilemma is even more serious when the conflict is of values, not just perceptions. Quiet residents of an urban neighborhood may see no difficulties with police harassment of their rowdier neighbors; the rowdies may legitimately claim that they have the right to be raucous as long as they end their loud parties before midnight and do not threaten other residents. In dealing with such a problem, police must balance the rights and needs of the two groups. This is hardly new—police have always had to balance the goals of serving the majority while guarding the liberties of the minority. Because it emphasizes public participation in defining and resolving problems, however, problem-oriented policing makes this balancing act all the more treacherous. It remains to be seen how the limits on police authority will be set; but it is certain that problem solving will require a new consensus on the role, authority, and limitations of the police in each jurisdiction that adopts it.[24]

The future: Beyond problem-oriented policing

As we have seen, problem-oriented policing is new. Traditional procedures die hard, problem-solving methods are still under development and no one knows for sure how successful the approach will be. As a result, no police agency has adopted the approach completely, and it will be a long time before many agencies do. On the other hand, problem-oriented policing is a realistic response to the limitations of traditional, incident-driven policing. It relies on a growing knowledge of the nature of crime and disorder, and it has been successful in a wide variety of police agencies, for a wide variety of urban crime and disorder problems. The problem-oriented approach seems to be where police work is going.

It also seems to be where other urban service agencies are going. Problem-oriented approaches have been implemented on an experimental basis in electric utilities,[25] urban transit authorities,[26] and recreation and parks departments.[27] Over the next few years, it is likely not only that there will be dramatic growth in the use of problem-solving techniques in municipal policing, but also that problem-oriented police officers will find problem-oriented firefighters, housing inspectors, and others to work with.

The growing use of problem-oriented approaches should help to reduce turf problems. As standard operating procedures become more flexible and decision making becomes decentralized, line officials may find that they owe as much allegiance to their colleagues from other agencies as they do to their own bureaucracies downtown. One natural method of institutionalizing these developments would be to adopt a matrix organizational structure. Neighborhood teams, consisting of members of the police, fire, public works, and other departments, would work together on a formal basis to deliver urban services. Although full implementation of a matrix is a long way off, the foundation for such a structure has already been laid in New York City. All urban service agencies are decentralized into eighty-eight districts with identical boundaries; citizens participate in agency decision making through community boards, which are a permanent part of the city government structure.[28]

A central element of problem-oriented policing is that administrative arrangements are less important than the activities that line officers undertake. But just as the centralized, control-oriented police structure helped police administrators to institutionalize incident-driven policing, so might a decentralized, team-based matrix help city managers to institutionalize problem-oriented urban service provision.

Such an interagency team approach would provide long-term benefits for the relationship between city government and the public, as well. More problem solvers would be available, with different backgrounds, viewpoints, and opportunities for contact with the public; this would improve the chances of early identification and complete analysis of problems. Because they would report to different bureaucracies, members of problem-solving teams would act as a check on one another, reducing many of the potential problems involved in the initial phases of problem solving described earlier. Finally, the teams would provide a unified contact point for frustrated citizens, who would otherwise be unable to negotiate their way through the city bureaucracy. If problem solving teams could be linked to community organizations, the opportunities for cooperative efforts would increase dramatically.

Benefits of innovations such as the interagency team, or matrix structure, are speculative. Problem-oriented policing is not. It provides a tested, practical approach for police agencies frustrated with putting Band-Aids on symptoms. By responding to recurring problems and by working with other agencies, businesses, and the public whenever possible, innovative police agencies have begun to develop an effective strategy for reducing crime and other troubling conditions in our cities.

1.   Philip J. Cook, "Research in Criminal Deterrence: Laying the Groundwork for the Second Decade," in Michael Tonry and Norval Morris, eds., *Crime and Justice: An Annual Review of Research*, vol. 4 (1980), 211–268.

2.   John E. Eck and William Spelman,

Problem Solving: Problem-Oriented Policing in Newport News (Washington, DC: Police Executive Research Forum, 1987).

3. J. Schnelle, R. Kirchner, J. Casey, P. Uselton, and M. McNees, "Patrol Evaluation Research: A Multiple-Baseline Analysis of Saturation Police Patrolling during Day and Night Hours," *Journal of Applied Behavior Analysis* 10 (1976): 33; George L. Kelling, Tony Pate, Duane Dieckman, and Charles E. Brown, *The Kansas City Preventive Patrol Experiment: A Technical Report* (Washington, DC: Police Foundation, 1974).

4. William Spelman and Dale K. Brown, *Calling the Police: Citizen Reporting of Serious Crime* (Washington, DC: Police Executive Research Forum, 1984).

5. John E. Eck, *Solving Crimes: The Investigation of Burglary and Robbery* (Washington, DC: Police Executive Research Forum, 1982); William Spelman, Michael Oshima, and George L. Kelling, *Crime Suppression and Traditional Police Tactics*, final report to the Florence V. Burden Foundation (Cambridge, MA: Program in Criminal Justice Policy and Management, Harvard University, 1985).

6. James M. Tien, James A. Simon, and Richard C. Larson, *An Alternative Approach in Police Patrol: The Wilmington Split-Force Experiment* (Washington, DC: U.S. Government Printing Office, 1978); John E. Eck, *Managing Case Assignments: The Burglary Investigation Decision Model Replication* (Washington, DC: Police Executive Research Forum, 1979); Thomas J. McEwen, Edward F. Connors, and Marcia I. Cohen, *Evaluation of the Differential Police Response Field Test* (Alexandria, VA: Research Management Associates, 1984).

7. Lawrence E. Cohen and Marcus Felson, "Social Change and Crime Rate Trends: A Routine Activity Approach," *American Sociological Review* 44 (1979): 588.

8. See, e.g., Thomas A. Reppetto, *Residential Crime* (Cambridge MA: Ballinger, 1974).

9. Jane Jacobs, *The Death and Life of Great American Cities* (New York: Vintage, 1961); Floyd J. Fowler, Jr., Mary Ellen McCalla, and Thomas W. Mangione, *Reducing Residential Crime and Fear: The Hartford Crime Prevention Program* (Washington, DC: U.S. Government Printing Office, 1979).

10. Stephanie W. Greenberg, William M. Rohe, and Jay R. Williams, *Safe and Secure Neighborhoods: Physical Characteristics and Informal Territorial Control in High- and Low-Crime Neighborhoods* (Washington, DC: U.S. Government Printing Office, 1982).

11. Alfred Blumstein, Jacqueline Cohen, Jeffrey A. Roth, and Christy A. Visher, *Criminal Careers and "Career Criminals,"* vol. 1 (Washington, DC: National Academy Press, 1986).

12. James F. Nelson, "Modeling Individual and Aggregate Victimization Rates," *Social Science Research* 13 (1984): 352.

13. Glenn L. Pierce, Susan Spaar, and LeBaron R. Briggs, *The Character of Police Work: Strategic and Tactical Implications* (Boston, MA: Center for Applied Social Research, Northeastern University, 1986); Lawrence W. Sherman, Patrick Gartin, and Michael Buerger, "Hot Spots of Predatory Crime: Routine Activities and the Criminology of Place," *Criminology* 27 (1984) 25–55.

14. Albert J. Reiss, Jr., "Victim Proneness in Repeat Victimization by Type of Crime," in Stephen E. Fienberg and Albert J. Reiss, Jr., *Indicators of Crime and Criminal Justice: Quantitative Studies* (Washington, DC: U.S. Government Printing Office, 1980), 41–53.

15. William Spelman, "The Incapacitation Benefits of Selected Criminal Justice Policies," Ph.D. diss., Committee on Public Policy, Harvard University, 1988.

16. Mark H. Moore, Susan R. Estrich, Daniel McGillis, and William

Spelman, *Dangerous Offenders: The Elusive Target of Justice* (Cambridge, MA: Harvard University Press, 1985).

17. Tien et al., *An Alternative Approach in Police Patrol.*
18. C. Ray Jeffery, *Crime Prevention through Environmental Design* (Beverly Hills, CA: Sage, 1971); Ronald V. Clarke and Derek B. Cornish, "Modeling Offenders' Decisions: A Framework for Research and Policy," in Michael Tonry and Norval Morris, eds., *Crime and Justice: An Annual Review of Research,* vol. 6 (1985), 147–185.
19. Oscar Newman, *Defensible Space: Crime Prevention through Environmental Design* (New York: MacMillan, 1972).
20. Greenberg et al., *Safe and Secure Neighborhoods.*
21. The three case studies described here are presented in more detail in the following: Vera Institute of Justice, "CPOP: Community Policing in Practice," unpublished paper (New York, 1988); Patrick T. Callahan, *Convenience Store Robberies: An Intervention Strategy by the City of Gainesville, Florida* (Gainesville: Gainesville Police Department, 1987); John E. Eck and William Spelman, "Who Ya Gonna Call? The Police as Problem-Busters," *Crime*

and *Delinquency* 33 (1987): 31–52.
22. Herman Goldstein, "Improving Policing: A Problem-Oriented Approach," *Crime and Delinquency* 25 (1979): 236–258.
23. John Mudd, *Neighborhood Services* (New Haven, CT: Yale University Press, 1984).
24. Herman Goldstein, "Toward Community-Oriented Policing: Potential Basic Requirements and Threshold Questions," *Crime and Delinquency* 33 (January 1987): 1–30.
25. John Francis Hird, "An Electric Utility," in W. Edwards Deming, ed., *Out of the Crisis* (Cambridge, MA: Center for Advanced Engineering Study, Massachusetts Institute of Technology, 1986), 238–245.
26. Harvey J. Brightman, *Group Problem Solving: An Improved Managerial Approach* (Atlanta, GA: Business Publishing Division, College of Business Administration, Georgia State University, 1988).
27. Joseph J. Bannon, *Problem Solving in Recreation and Parks* (Englewood Cliffs, NJ: Prentice-Hall, 1972).
28. Peter Marcuse, "Neighborhood Policy and the Distribution of Power: New York City's Community Boards," *Policy Studies Journal* 16 (Winter 1987): 277–289.

Rethinking Drug Enforcement Policy: An Interview with Arnold S. Trebach

Peter Dodenhoff

Over the course of a long and prolific career, American University Professor Arnold S. Trebach has made an imprint on numerous areas of criminal justice, from serving as a consultant to the U.S. Department of Justice to administering a criminal defense project for the National Legal Aid and Defender Association. In 1987, Trebach's work took another bold step forward when he founded the Drug Policy Foundation, which is described as "an independent think tank devoted to promoting peaceful and effective drug policy reform."

Trebach's views of the war on drugs are shaped in part by the conclusion that the war has claimed as its victims some of society's most pitiful members—the seriously ill, who are denied access to narcotic pain relief—as well as society's protectors, the police establishment. To Trebach, the police role in combating drugs is roughly akin to sending Marines into Beirut: The mission is fuzzy and extremely difficult. He echoes the notion of pioneering police thinker August Vollmer that police work in the drug field corrodes the entire police institution, subjecting officers to enormous temptations to violate the law in order to enforce it. Says Trebach, "I view my friends in law enforcement with great admiration, and I worry about them."

LAW ENFORCEMENT NEWS: *In a nutshell, why is America losing the war on drugs, as the title of your newest book* [The Great Drug War] *suggests?*

TREBACH: Well, for a variety of reasons, not least of which is that the whole concept of a "war" on drugs is inappropriate. There's no way you can have a war on a chemical. What you really have is a war on a

Excerpted from *Law Enforcement News*, April 30, 1988, issue, with the permission of John Jay College of Criminal Justice, City University of New York.

significant segment of the American people. Roughly one in four Americans used an illegal drug within the past 12 months, so what you're saying is that we're going to go to war against 25 percent of the American people. That's a civil war. If it's only a war on rhetoric, then it's just great political fun. But it's becoming a real war, more or less a sectarian or civil war, and we should tremble to think where such attitudes could take us.

That's the first part of the problem. Another reason why we're losing the war is because we do not distinguish between the legal drugs and the illegal drugs with any degree of rationality. We act as if there is a distinction, when in fact there isn't. To say we're going to war against the illegal drugs, which really are not a great health threat on the whole to the American people, and virtually ignore the legal drugs is irrational.

Another reason why it's failing is that we have never shown any great ability at Prohibition. We failed at it in the twenties, we are now failing at it, and there's no evidence whatsoever that we can succeed at it in the future, even if we turn the society into a police state.

LEN: *If cost were no object, is the war winnable?*

TREBACH: I know of no way to do it. [If I were appointed drug czar and given a huge budget] I would have to say to the President, "I'm more stunned than flattered that you asked me, but I would not know how to use those 10 to 20 billion dollars to successfully win a war as that war is currently defined." There's nothing in our history, nothing in the history of any other major country to suggest that it can be done.

LEN: *So you're suggesting, then, that winning this war, if in fact it's feasible, would entail costs that go far beyond monetary expenditures?*

TREBACH: Yes. What most objective observers have seen is that even to push the war rationally and logically further down the current path will go very far in the direction of creating a police state. We are doing that already and it's not working. President Nixon's commission on marijuana and drug abuse said that it is possible to increase the level of police power and military power applied to the drug war, but this could well mean the invasion of many of the most cherished rights of Americans.

LEN: *That commission recommended that current marijuana laws be replaced by a decriminalized approach. Why were those recommendations written off?*

TREBACH: Well, first remember that every major commission that has studied marijuana has come to remarkably similar conclusions.

Every one of them went out there expecting to find how marijuana was tearing up the people. Each of them concluded that while marijuana was not harmless—and I agree, it's not harmless—it simply did not present a great threat, on the whole, to the people of the country where it was being used. They said, "We looked at the evidence, and though marijuana can be a difficult problem for many people, on the whole it's not a very damaging presence in our society, and we should be somewhat more lenient with it." As in the past, it's the last thing the people who set up the commission wanted to hear. [This type of report] was politically unacceptable, and that's been our problem with most of the drugs. We set up political standards for science, for objective research, and when the science and objective research don't comport, we go with politics rather than with science.

LEN: *Some argue that in the context of the war on drugs, the object lessons of Prohibition appear to have been lost in the shuffle.*

TREBACH: [Many people say] "How can you compare this with Prohibition? It's just not the same." Well, alcohol was a drug that was widely accepted and we attempted to take it away from the people. And also, it wasn't that harmful on the whole. Moreover, they say that Prohibition had a good impact. It controlled the overall use of alcohol. They say that when we removed Prohibition, alcohol use nearly doubled. So there are a host of reasons, I think, why we don't see exact similarities and why, indeed, many people liked Prohibition. I see the situation quite the opposite. Number one, I think that what we are doing now is very close to what we did in the twenties, except that now it's more savage. In the twenties, we did not go after users; we went after sellers and racketeers. Now we're saying that going after the user is the answer to the problem. Second, the analogy in terms of police corruption, the crime of the traffickers, the erosion of civil liberties, all of these are precise. If we were to legalize some of these drugs, it's possible that use might go up. So, I think the analogies with Prohibition are very good, and in the end I am mystified as to why people don't say "This is just like Prohibition," and we should say, as we did in the thirties, that alcohol is bad but Prohibition is worse.

LEN: *As you mentioned, there are those who suggest that the moment drugs were legalized, should they be, use would go up, perhaps significantly. Others, however, have surmised that use might actually decrease, simply because the curiosity of trying something that's illegal will have been removed, and young people might find the idea of drug experimentation to be rather ho-hum.*

TREBACH: The evidence would suggest the possibility of both responses. As I pointed out in *The Great Drug War*,[1] clearly the experience of Holland and Alaska with respect to marijuana, which are really the only two examples we have of a very lenient approach to any of the illicit drugs, suggests that nothing terrible would happen if we removed some of the criminal sanctions. In Alaska, as I documented, there's been no dramatic change in drug use. Illicit drug use is very high in Alaska, but there's nothing to indicate that it went up after the *Raven* decision in 1975 [which granted Alaskans the right to grow and possess marijuana in homes for personal use], and no indication of an increase in auto accidents or anything of this nature. So it's legal, not just decriminalized. In Holland, you find that while it's illegal, the authorities virtually do not enforce the law against possession or small sales. The youth of Holland can buy all the drugs they want, and you have indications of a drop from the old days. Any survey of Dutch use that I've studied shows that one-half of 1 percent use marijuana daily. That's in a country where the kids can get all the pot they want, right off the menus of coffee houses. In this country, as I found when I wrote the book, it's about 4 to 5 percent. In other words, it's about ten times as much in this country.

LEN: Any thoughts as to what that might be attributable to?

TREBACH: I suspect that it's partly that the Dutch rely more on cultural, familial and social controls, and they are generally a very conservative people. It's not that they look upon the use of marijuana lightly, but on the other hand they don't like the idea of the cops arresting their children. So for them the major controls are where they should be: in the family, in the church, in the culture. Also, I think that Dutch youths are bored with marijuana; there's nothing deviant about it. Society is already saying you can get all the pot you want, although we don't think you're wise in doing so.

LEN: You refer to the alternative to a war on drugs as "drug peace." If the war on drugs is not winnable, is the alternative, as some have said, mere surrender?

TREBACH: Not at all. My hope is that peace means we can now work out our conflicts, which will certainly be there, within the framework of the peaceful methods of a democracy. That means you seek out compromises and the middle ground between the extremes. I called it "drug peace" because I think people use "drug war" like it's one word—like "damn Yankees" used to be. So, if you need a word, call it "drug peace," and let's say we're going to approach this in a peaceful way and seek compassionate compromises. Well, what could that involve? A whole series of things, it turns out. For example, one of the first things we'd do is to recognize who the true victims of the war are, and help them. And I think most people would agree that some of the most pitiful victims of the war are sick people, people denied heroin for pain relief in cancer cases, people denied marijuana for relief of the agonies of chemotherapy, people with glaucoma who are denied the help that marijuana can provide in preventing the onset of glaucoma-related blindness, people with multiple sclerosis, where marijuana might well help the tremors and the shaking and the lack of control that comes with that disease. There's no reason in the world why sick people should be denied because we think dope fiends will eventually get their hands on the drugs.

LEN: *Or that the sick people will themselves become drug addicts as a result of using these substances?*

TREBACH: That's right. That should be irrelevant. In addition, I would like us to start thinking of narcotics addicts as sick people with a bad habit. One compromise might be to offer them a wide array of affordable, legal treatments that could range from the standard drug-free treatment to oral methadone and on to other oral drugs, all of which are now illegal for maintenance, and then on to injectable drugs. We must consider the possibility of providing injectable drugs and clean needles, so that a new compromise goal might be to start saying that we accept the presence of injecting addicts in our society—although we wish they weren't here—and our job is to keep them alive and to create healthy injecting addicts. That, of course, just shakes a lot of experts up, and it is politically unacceptable. But we'd better start accepting that, because the major engine for transmission of AIDS is not the homosexual couple, but the heterosexual injecting addict.

LEN: *What's your personal position on the use of drugs, whether licit or illicit? You don't appear to be sanctioning such use.*

TREBACH: That's right. My feeling is that we'd be better off if none of us used any of these things. So personally, I would support total abstinence from any drug, including alcohol. It would be a great thing. I don't smoke, drink or do anything of that nature myself. But that's personal. The fact that my neighbor may be doing something totally different with alcohol or any other drug is, in a democracy, none of my damn business, in a way. I don't want my neighbors coming over my fence and throwing out their beer bottles or their needles, and thank God they don't. But I think there ought to be a lot of room for individual drug preferences. That's not approval: that's accepting the reality of the many-hued desires that people have.

LEN: *Is there anything in the way of a distinction between licit and illicit drugs in their potential for harm, let's say?*

TREBACH: It's not so much the potential, because potential comes out of experiments with rats. If you looked at experiments with rats, no one should be drinking diet cola, because rats seem to die from saccharin. If you look at illicit drugs in terms of the reality, in terms of the way people use them, I see an enormously greater threat from the legal drugs than from the illegal drugs. The question that always comes up is, "Would this be true if you loosened the law?" My guess is yes. The nature of tobacco, for example, is that you use it a great deal. The nature of marijuana is that you don't use it a great deal—even though I suspect it's at least as bad as tobacco in terms of organic harm. Over 50 million people fix more than 20 times a day with tobacco cigarettes. There are very few people who smoke more than three joints a day of marijuana, and that would be a great amount of that drug. Generally speaking, marijuana is used much less than once a day. If marijuana were legal, I don't see people using it much more. So, on the whole, I see a much greater threat overall from the legal drugs than from the illegal drugs, even if we turned around and loosened some of the restrictions on the illegal drugs.

LEN: *Wouldn't legalization carry with it the implicit suggestion that the government is getting into the business of drug dealing? Or could the matter be opened up to private entrepreneurship under a regulatory scheme such as we now have with alcoholic beverages?*

TREBACH: We ought to look at our experiment with alcohol and learn from that. When we allowed the states to legalize alcohol, we did not carry with that national campaign enough warnings about alcohol. I think where research ought to be going in this field is along the lines of what new control schemes make sense beyond prohibition. Because if anybody thinks that one day we're going to simply be rid of all the laws and everything will be fine, they're as mistaken as the drug warriors. What we need is to think out new, more effective laws and policies. So my hope would be that we would provide for a wide array of experiments in the states on how to control drugs. A good part of that ought to provide for private control, but I wouldn't object in those states with state package stores for liquor if they sold some of the drugs there. Sell the drugs in the store, make sure they're sold only to adults, make sure they have health warnings on them, because all of these drugs are dangerous. There should be tax stamps on the drugs; we should make sure they're pure, that they meet all the FDA requirements for safety and efficacy. I can see that kind of scheme in some states. In other states, I can see drugs sold in private stores as well, so long as there were health warnings on the packages, so long as purity was assured, so long as it was clear that there were age limits and tax stamps, so you can earn a lot of money that's now going to criminals.

LEN: What would be the technical distinctions between legalization of narcotic drugs and decriminalization?

TREBACH: In the end, I think these words are not terribly important. But to me, decriminalization means that in the law you have virtually ignored possession, or you're treating it like a traffic offense. You go in and you pay a fine. Legalization, on the other hand, would mean that the drug is fully legal for possession and sale. In general, I would accept any approach here that says this is no longer a matter for the criminal law and the police. I don't care how it's done. In Holland, remember, marijuana is still illegal, and the way in which they've achieved their progress is through the structured use of police and prosecutorial discretion. So in effect they've decriminalized it in a *de facto* way. They've said, in effect, that if you have possession of small amounts, or if you are a small dealer, we are not going to prosecute. So I would accept any approach—decriminalization, legalization, or *de facto* decriminalization—that reduces the actual involvement of the criminal law, the police and the prisons.

LEN: For historical background, what brought about the criminalization of the current array of illegal drugs, such as heroin, cocaine, or marijuana? After all, they haven't always been perceived as criminal problems.

TREBACH: Well, we're strip-searching everybody coming in from Asia and from Mexico, and the drugs are flooding down the Canadian border. What do we do now? Well, we close the Canadian border. How many divisions would it take to close the Canadian border? Well, you might say we could close the Canadian border, but then drugs might start coming in through Florida again. So let's close down Florida. You begin to recognize that we simply can't do it. It isn't like you're trying to prevent an invasion by several divisions of Russian troops. You are trying to prevent people from smuggling very small packages of goods, some of which, because of our drug wars, are now worth $10,000 for a little bit of cocaine about the size of a couple of cigarette packs. Never in the history of the world has the military been able to prevent that kind of traffic from occurring. So, in the end, forgetting the Constitution and forgetting our tradition, I see nothing to suggest that the military could even do it.

LEN: One other approach that has been suggested involves redirecting the war on drugs to the demand side of the equation, given the absence of genuine, meaningful successes in the war on drug traffickers. Would such an effort hold any great promise?

TREBACH: Again, put aside the Constitution and all our petty, technical concerns about such things as decency and privacy. I see no evidence that it would work. There's nothing to indicate that you could control this even in a totalitarian state. In some of my earlier writings, I pointed out the experience of revolutionary Iran. You had a situation where the roving executioner of the revolution assumed the right, with official support, to put somebody found to be using or selling drugs up against the nearest wall and shoot him. Yet the use and trafficking of drugs continued, and when the executioner was criticized for not controlling it, he replied, "If I had to shoot everyone who had five grams of heroin, it would involve shooting 5,000 people." And then he added the classic words, "And this would be difficult." It's hard to shoot 5,000 people, and of course we're dealing with many more than that. So I see no evidence in the history of totalitarian countries that this attack on users has ever been successful. And now that we've started to do a little bit, we've virtually lost the prison option. Our prisons are now so full that we have virtually no room. You can put a few big-time criminals away, but any notion that you can fill the jails with misdemeanants for possession is preposterous, because at a given point you simply have run out of room, and exhausted the prison option. And we pretty much have done that now.

LEN: Wouldn't urinalysis drug screening hold some promise for scaring people away from drug use?

TREBACH: Well, that would be the major way in which you'd go about getting at the users. And to an extent it will work; it will scare some people away. But remember what you're going to come up with, for the most part, because of the nature in which the drugs are secreted from the body. Ninety-five percent of the time you'll come up with occasional marijuana users. This will have very little effect on cocaine and heroin users, because generally the stuff is secreted from the body very rapidly. If you have a wild cocaine party on Friday night, probably by Monday noon you would test reasonably clean. Nobody tests for alcohol, or for tobacco. And when they tried mass urinalysis in the Army, the impact was to genuinely discourage marijuana smoking among certain parts of the population, but in many cases alcohol use went up, tobacco use was unaffected, and I suspect, although I can't prove it, that cocaine use and the use of other hard drugs might have increased. So in the end, I don't see this as having much of an impact, or as a victory. We're going to scare people away from occasional marijuana use and perhaps encourage the use of other drugs.

LEN: Just to narrow the focus a bit, what about those agencies or com-

panies that employ drug testing in cases where they have some reasonable suspicion that an employee is under the influence?

TREBACH: I think the way to go with urinalysis drug screening is to say that this is a new technology and we should use it where appropriate. If you've got prisoners in custody I think you can use it. If you've got addicts in a treatment program you can use it. And, in an employment situation, if you've got some reasona ble suspicion that an employee is abusing drugs or alcohol, I think you can call him in and talk to him. An employer should have a right to do that. More than that, I think there is a right to a drug-free workplace. As an employer, you should have the right to say you don't want anything consumed on your premises, and that would include alcohol and tobacco. I would fully support that. I fully support the idea of drug-free airplanes. But when you move beyond those kinds of narrowly defined situations and go into the mass specter haunting this country—mass random tests of bodily fluids—then [you violate] every principle that this country holds sacred.

LEN: Has the latest war on drugs given rise to any positive aspects, in your estimation? One that comes readily to mind as a possibility might be the increase in drug-abuse education efforts, or the "Just Say No" campaign.

TREBACH: I think there are some good things there. More and more youngsters are saying, "Hey, there may be something wrong with these drugs, and I shouldn't take 'em just because my friends like to." More and more are accepting the idea that they can say "no." I like "Just Say No" as one approach to dealing with the problem. But the difficulty is that it's not enough. You need other approaches. In the end, we must recognize that the greatest controls are familial, cultural, personal, ethical. What we've got to say is that we must build up honest education and treatment as the major ways in which we control drug abuse. So, to the extent to which the current approaches have helped build that up, fine. But they certainly haven't gone far enough. "Just Say No" suggests "Do as I say and you'll be okay." Whereas most American kids will say, "Just say no? Why? Why not say yes?" They want more information. I retreat to Jeffersonian principles here. Over time, on balance, the people in a democracy make more right decisions than wrong ones. And the way they do is by being provided with the full array of conflicting facts. We do not provide them with that in the drug field. The government lies about drugs, and therefore, when people find out the lies, they're not prepared to believe the government or to believe experts. We have got to provide the full array of conflicting facts and allow people to make up their own minds on the basis of all those facts. And we've got to see to it that any person in trouble with any drug—legal or illegal—gets affordable treatment as often as needed. Those are the two major ways in which we'll come through this mess.

LEN: *Can familial or social controls, be it "Just Say No" or any other approach, tend toward unacceptable extremes, in your view?*

TREBACH: Yes, and that's the problem. If we are to say to kids, "If you have a beer, you will become an alcoholic," or tell a boy that he will grow breasts, or tell a girl that she will not be able to conceive, or you will lose your mind, people will tell you that you're crazy. But we say that about illegal drugs. We say that if you have a marijuana joint or two, you will go on to heroin or smoke crack or snort cocaine. You will become a degenerate and be destroyed by it all. People will say, "That's not true. I had a joint last night, and I'm an A student and I'm doing fine." We must accept the fact that large numbers of American youth and American adults use illegal drugs quite responsibly. [Officials and experts] don't want to hear that.

LEN: *So in your estimation there is such a thing as responsible drug use?*

TREBACH: Absolutely. I say that not because I approve of drug use, and not because I urge people to do it, or because I want people to do it. But that's what the facts say, and as a scholar I must report what I find.

LEN: *Yet there are other scholars or researchers who would lay out their own facts to draw the conclusion that your view is patently absurd, that marijuana is the gateway to the wild kingdom of drug abuse.*

TREBACH: They may feel that way, but I look at the data and I have to report honestly that I don't see it that way. It's in the government's own facts and figures. For example, the government reports that at least 60 million people have tried marijuana once or more. If marijuana was such a corrupter or gateway to other drugs, then the number of people using the other drugs would be astronomical. In fact, the government data indicate that the number of people who have used the other drugs are a tiny percentage of those who have used marijuana. So when I look at all the data, I see nothing in the gateway or escalation theory.

LEN: *I believe you have also hypothesized that marijuana may in fact serve as a stopping point for people who try it, perhaps continue using it occasionally, and conclude that there's no need to satisfy their curiosity about drugs any further than marijuana.*

TREBACH: Right. What I found—and this is again based on government data—is that the pattern of marijuana use for most people is that they try it in their mid-teens, and they may, by their late teens, be into intense daily use, even abuse. By the time they hit their early twenties, they start to taper off, and by the time they're twenty-six it has virtually disappeared from their lives. It has no effect on them and they don't go on to anything else. Once they hit twenty-six, people tend to become less deviant in every way. They start to change, perhaps as early as twenty-two in some cases, and the change includes drug use. So there's no indication of a great explosion of drug use arising out of even intense marijuana use as a teenager or a person in his early twenties.

LEN: In The Great Drug War, *you describe law enforcement personnel as being among the victims of the drug wars. In what ways?*

TREBACH: A lot of police officers I know say, "It's the law, and I'm going to enforce it." I want them to do that, but more and more are also saying, "We've got to think of different ways of dealing with this, because this is not working." The great August Vollmer said that police have no role in the vice field.[2] It just corrodes their institution. I find a number of street cops coming to me and saying that we've got to do something different.

One other thing has struck me. It may look like personal failing when you see these corrupt police, but we say to the cops, in effect, go out and work in this drug and crime sewer, and when they do bad things, we say to them, "You smell like you've been working in a sewer." We created the sewer for them, and unless we change it, we're still going to find corrupt cops, cops who violate the law in order to enforce it, cops becoming increasingly ineffective in other areas of law enforcement because we've got them mired in the dangerous and corrupt drug field.

LEN: In order to effect any kind of change in the American posture toward drugs, it would seem that you'd need pockets of "drug-peace activism" among elected officials as well. Do you see any of that?

TREBACH: Let me tell you something that's really remarkable. I set up this Drug Policy Foundation, which is a little independent think-tank, and I am simply amazed at the number of officials coming to me and saying, "You can't use my name, but you're right about drugs." It's constant, and it involves both elected and executive officials. I got a call the other day from an official of the Department of Justice, who said, "I just want you to know that I am following developments in the Drug Policy Foundation with great interest. Keep me on your mailing list. I can't say anything about this, but I want to encourage you very much." Then he hangs up after leaving that message on our machine. This is common. Through an intermediary, I had a member of the U.S. House of Representatives say, "I've got a very tough district, and I can't say anything in your favor, but I want you to know that I'm with you, and you've got to work to the point of changing public opinion so I can say this openly." We don't feel so lonely at the foundation anymore, because more and more we're getting that kind of encouragement, and less and less criticism.

LEN: There has been a marked increase in the number of newspaper columnists who have come out with positions favoring an alternative to the war on drugs. To what might you attribute this surge of objection to current policy?

TREBACH: I think that all of us who have been objecting for the last many years can claim some credit. But, in addition, I have ultimate faith in the good common sense of the American people. I think that when they start looking at the facts, they start to say, "Egads, this darn thing isn't working. It may sound good, but it doesn't work." In the end, I think that's what will doom this thing. As with alcohol, people said alcohol is bad but Prohibition is worse. I think they're going to say that.

Let me tell you what I hope doesn't happen though. I hope that we don't attack getting rid of the drug laws with the same zeal that we've used enforcing them. That would be terrible. I don't want people just changing the drug laws and saying, as they did with alcohol, "Whoopee, we're safe because the government changed the law." It ought to be very cautious experimentation. We should start with marijuana. We should say to the states that we're going to take the same approach with marijuana now as we took with alcohol in 1933, and allow the states to experiment. Once they do that, they should experiment with a wide array of control measures that really are cautious in the manner that they're done and evaluated and adjusted. And the clear message would be a contradictory one: We're making it legal, but we're not saying you should use it. We're saying that if you feel you must, fine, but there are many reasons why you shouldn't use any drugs at all. There should be honest education about the dangers of all the drugs, and—here's the part that will hurt—honest education about how to use them responsibly. That will hurt, but that's the only way in which we will achieve controls, because the controls are in the human being's sense of ethics and sense of health, and in the human being's parents and family and culture. Not in the cops. You've got to get new ideas in there, and among those new ideas must be responsible use.

Let me give some examples of what I mean by responsible use. Some of the best ways to use a drug responsibly are to use it with some ceremony, and never to use it alone. By ceremony, I suppose if you want to use a drug during a Sunday football game, that makes sense, whether you drink beer or whatever. If every lunch, or every time you watch TV, you are smoking a joint, snorting cocaine, or drinking beer, I think you've got a problem. Another notion would be never to use drugs every day. That's responsible use. Most people abuse the legal drugs. They smoke a cigarette and have coffee for breakfast. I think it's a bad idea if you do it every day. I think it's much more responsible if you don't do it every day. Another rule would be never to use a drug with addicts. That can have a bad influence on you; you could adopt their patterns. So that's what I mean by learning the lessons of responsible use.

LEN: *If the answer to the drug war is to call it off, to put it in simple terms, is there a point in time after which it is no longer possible to call things off, simply because drug traffickers are so powerful that no degree of decriminalization will make a difference?*

TREBACH: I don't think so. I think we're all united in wanting to see drug traffickers caught. I don't think any sensible person opposes that. I support the police, and many people support the police in their going after organized crime syndicates that traffic in drugs, or any kind of predatory drug trafficker. But my support has nothing to do with my belief in that action as a way to control drug use. To these organized criminal syndicates, drugs are irrelevant. They'd sell peanut butter if there were that much profit in it. So by changing the rules on drugs, I have every belief that these groups will be into some thing else. There are plenty of lucrative things for people in organized crime to get involved in.

But the big point here is to emphasize that we can compromise on this. We can come up with sensible, humane methods of dealing with this problem that are not at the extremes on either side of the argument. That's what we should be reaching for. We should be seeking out those new positions in the middle ground. That's the big message.

1. Arnold S. Trebach, *The Great Drug War* (New York: McMillan, 1987).
2. While generally an advocate of rigorous law enforcement, Vollmer believed strongly that police efforts to enforce vice laws were doomed to failure. In 1936, disheartened by the corruption bred by Prohibition, he wrote in his classic *The Police and Modern Society* (Berkeley, CA: University of California Press, 1936; and Montclair, NJ: Patterson-Smith Reprints, 1971, pp. 81-88) that: "The difficulties surrounding vice repression arise because of the means employed by society in dealing with this problem. Repression by legislation against the various forms of evil has failed miserably in its execution. The desirability of a moral community is incontestable. The suffering, degradation, dependency,

neglect of home and children, debauchery of youth, and the time and money spent on supervising the hellholes are proof enough that vice should be eradicated. But legislative enactment has never been, and never will be, a panacea for moral turpitude. As long as the immoral qualities remain unaltered, just so long will the possessor of these qualities behave in a manner adverse to the moral code, and it is absurd, and stupid as well, to think that fines and jail sentences can change the character of an individual. 'Laws have never been a substitute for human virtues.' The character of a community is but a reflection of the character of its residents, and no matter how many laws are on the statute books, enforcement can go no further than the citizens will permit. And that permission does not go very far. The unwillingness of the people to face the facts about vice, their inability to exercise reason and judgment in dealing with it, and their faithful and reverential devotion to the idea that the problem can be solved with the passing of repressive laws, have been the greatest handicaps to vice as one of the most important problems of society.

"Vice can be overcome, if at all, only by educative processes. It is axiomatic that any law, to be enforceable, must be unreservedly supported by the sentiment of a whole people. The entire community affected must genuinely believe that a prohibited act is morally and socially wrong before the enforcement of the law designed for the elimination of that act will be successful. Extremists never see conditions as they exist, especially if it is a problem concerned with vice. They are blinded by their prejudices, their as-sertions are usually based on desire or theory rather than on facts, and their biased attitude is only the logical outcome of their gross ignorance of the true conditions. Rarely are reformers capable of realizing how many are the ramifications of vice in a community . . .

"[T]here is also the very great and very definite injury that results through the diversion of the police from the investigation of major crimes and the apprehension of professional criminals . . . major crimes must go unsolved and major criminals remain unapprehended . . .

"Another handicap to police effectiveness in the enforcement of laws against vice is the fact that, in the prosecution of vice-law violators, the rules of evidence favor the habitues of the underworld. The complete case against the person involved cannot be presented, because of the rules governing the admissibility of evidence; also, much of the information that is presented is discredited by jurors because of the objectionable manner in which it is obtained. Evidence can rarely be gathered by the policeman himself; he must use paid informers for this purpose. Because of this fact, and because of the revolting methods used to get evidence, the defense attorney is afforded ample opportunity with which to attack the character of the informer, and juries often hesitate to convict. To obtain the services of honest and incorruptible, jury-proof, vice informers, policemen generally concede, is almost impossible. Experience has shown that frequently the person who will accept payment from the police to inform upon prostitutes, gamblers, and liquor violators, will also accept payment from these persons to deceive the police."

A Law Enforcement Response to Legalizing Illicit Drugs

————————— Edward J. Tully and Margo Bennett

Editor's note: The authors wrote this paper on behalf of the FBI Academy's National Executive Institute Associates' Major City Chiefs of Police group. The paper has the unanimous endorsement of the Major City Chiefs, but is not an official statement of the FBI, the DEA, or any single police department or individual police executive.

Those who cannot remember the past are condemned to repeat it.
—George Santayana
Life of Reason, Volume 1

When the question of legalizing illicit drugs was raised at the October 1988 meeting of the Major City Chiefs (an organization consisting of 48 chief executive officers of the largest law enforcement organizations in the United States and Canada), the chiefs responded with disappointment, having believed that the merits of this issue had long since been settled. Their next step was to encourage the preparation of an appropriate response, reflecting the general thinking of the law enforcement community.

The objective of the following article is to present the reasonable legalization arguments and provide the persuasive rebuttals known to law enforcement officials. Our purpose is not to chill debate, or to demean those who are, in good faith, calling for some aspect of legalization. Neither should this be viewed as an attempt to glorify, justify or rationalize law enforcement's efforts to control drug problems during the past 20 years or so. We have made many mistakes in the past and will probably make more in the future. When these errors occur, we encourage the community to call them to our attention so that we can make appropriate corrections and adjustments.

Both sides of the legalization argument agree that North America has a serious drug abuse problem that involves both legal and illegal substances. The stated goals of both sides are to protect individual rights, reduce general and violent crime, promote the mental and physical health of the people and ensure a better quality of life for all citizens. Thus, the discussion should center on the path we take to ensure that our mutual objectives are met. The law enforcement community argues that legalization advocates propose dangerous experiments in social policy. In our view, the legalization of illicit drugs promises no significant benefit to anyone in our society. Therefore, we view the experiments as risks that we should not entertain.

Following are basic arguments presented by proponents of legalization.

Argument 1: The protection of individual rights

The central, underlying theme of many arguments to legalize illicit drugs is that individuals in a free society have a right to make their own choices, even if their exercise of liberty leads to their own destruction. This argument was offered by Dr. Ethan Nadelman in the Summer 1988 issue of *Public Interest*. "Legalization is . . . a recognition of the right to make . . . choices free of the fear of criminal sanction." Once again, as often in the past, the debate over legalization centers around the delicate balance between the liberty and rights of individuals and the well-being of the community. Americans have frequently held that as long as an individual's behavior does not adversely affect others, then he ought to be free to do as he chooses. This position safeguards free speech, freedom of religion, freedom of association and the freedom to live a reasonable lifestyle. The conflict comes when an individual's action threatens the community. If the community decides that the potential threat to the citizenry legitimately overrides the freedom exercised by the individual, it handles the problem through laws or cultural norms, or both.

In order for the "individual rights" argument to succeed, the proponents of legalization must successfully argue that the abuse of currently illicit drugs does not pose a significant threat. In practice, proponents offer the rationale that drugs are not harmful; that many individuals who use them are perfectly competent; that users and addicts are not primarily to blame for their actions while under the influence; that actions of the community to protect itself are more of a threat to the public good than the actions of drug abusers;

and, finally, that there would be fewer social problems if current criminal sanctions were lifted and education and treatment were emphasized instead.

No one denies the importance of drug prevention, education and treatment. But the real issues are (1) whether society and government have the authority to protect the public from the harmful acts of drug abusers and other persons who would do it harm either intentionally or otherwise; (2) whether society should protect an individual from himself; and (3) what measure—or combination of measures—is acceptable, in terms of diminished individual rights, to promote the common welfare?

In response to the first issue, all sides agree, in general terms, that certain aspects of drug abuse (violence to others, for example) pose a significant threat to our society and that, in these cases, society does have a fundamental right to take measures to protect itself from danger.

Second, American and Canadian societies have a long history of taking appropriate measures to protect people from their own unwise actions. They have established mandatory social security regulations, seat belt laws and child labor laws, among others.

Finally, America's traditions of government and social policy are based on the recognition that individuals are responsible for the consequences of their actions. Some legalization advocates have sought to shift responsibility from the individual, blaming society for drug use. Thus, a person who freely chooses to become drug dependent is excused of any blame for acts or consequences. Usually the first to be blamed are the poor parents, who must obviously have erred in parenting. Next in line are the schools, the churches and the individual's peers. Finally, the laws are blamed. If this argument is accepted, it follows that the drug-induced actions should be legalized on the logical assumption that the attendant problems will fade.

Proponents of "individual rights" have used this argument in the past with respect to sexual conduct, speech and a host of other issues, successfully at times and unsuccessfully at others. In the case of drug abuse, however, it is difficult to accept the argument that individuals must not be held accountable for their lifestyles. A large number of our citizens have freely chosen to ignore the law and to engage in activities that are a threat not only to themselves, but also to the community.

In this situation, the law was not wrong, unjust or an unacceptable infringement on individual rights. The responsibility of government is to do what it can do to ensure that its citizens are able to enjoy and exercise their very considerable freedoms. Government "of the people, by the people and for the people" requires a population physically and mentally able to make prudent decisions.

Argument 2: Punitive measures lead to violence, corruption and crime

According to legalization advocates, the law enforcement approach and the use of punitive and repressive measures have led to violence, corruption of public officials and a significant increase in general crime.

It is true that levels of violence, general crime and, to a lesser extent, corruption of public officials have increased over the past 20 years. These trends can be tied directly or indirectly to legal or illegal drug abuse. However, to suggest that the increase in crime levels is caused by the illegality of some substances, or marketing practices, stretches logic to the breaking point. It requires acceptance of the implausible claim that individuals who choose to use or distribute drugs, and subsequently become involved in additional unlawful activities, somehow bear no responsibility. The government is blamed because it has made the ingested substance illegal, difficult to obtain or expensive.

This argument is naive. One reason people use mind-altering drugs is because they want to feel good. Individuals who continue drug use do so because they want to, or until they reach a point where they lose individual control over their lives. Up to this point, use of drugs is strictly voluntary. Thus, the inexorable drift to addiction on the part of some drug users is the result of a multitude of individual choices made over time.

The violence and criminal behaviors exhibited by people under the influence of drugs are not motivated by legal sanctions. The law, per se, does not cause their behavior. Individuals choose their behavior. If that behavior violates a law, harms another person or corrupts a public official, it is not reasonable to blame the law. We do not blame the law in the case of the bank robber, wife beater or shoplifter. In reality, most individuals involved in criminal activity are either oblivious to or contemptuous of the law. Social rules are for other people, not for them. In our experience, there are few drug addicts, drug dealers or drug-induced criminals who would argue that the law, or law enforcement, caused their behavior. More to the point of the argument is that few drug traffickers would "go straight" if narcotics were legalized.

One final note on the corruption of public officials: It is true that present illegal drug activities have provided the wealth needed to corrupt police officers, judges or others involved in the criminal justice system. But this should not be viewed as part of the drug problem. It is a problem of having public servants who are susceptible to corruption and hence not fit for public service. Whether the motivation for corruption is drugs, money or power, the problem of corruption is a problem of character. In the final analysis, the problem of public corruption can be solved if we first select men and women of good character to be public servants.

The proponents of "individual rights" as the centerpiece in their argument for the legalization of drugs place a high value on an individual's right to choose. The law enforcement community acknowledges the importance of individual rights and liberty, but considers the probable common good to be endangered by the legalization of drugs. We hold that it is destructive of the common good to legitimize patterns of behavior with drugs by which individuals become a threat to others and an enormous community liability. Thus, we reject the argument that current drug laws have made the drug problem worse. What has made the problem worse are individuals who made some very poor choices.

Argument 3: Supply reduction policies have failed

Proponents of legalization insist that despite law enforcement's best efforts, the supply of drugs has increased, substance purity has increased and price has decreased. Thus, they argue, law enforcement has failed. This is far from true; and it misleads reflections about wise social policy. Of all illicit drugs, only cocaine has increased in availability and purity at decreased prices. Marijuana, heroin and hashish have remained relatively stable and high priced, which is the objective of supply reduction. The principal reason cocaine has become more widely available is that the cocaine cartels have a huge supply of the easily stored drug which they have been dumping on the North American market in order to increase demand. Despite recent events in Afghanistan, Iran and Lebanon which have wiped out previously supportive law enforcement activities in those nations, our interdiction efforts have kept the supplies of other drugs fairly stable.

On the other hand, to claim that law enforcement has been completely successful with its reduction efforts is not justified. Law enforcement now recognizes that we will not be able to eliminate the flow of illicit drugs into North America. The demand for drugs is too high and the ease of smuggling drugs over the borders is too well known for our efforts to be totally successful. However, capitulation in this area means a significant increase in drugs, or in the case of several countries which have de facto capitulation, the possible loss of the entire country. The recognition of this fact has led law enforcement to open a second front by devoting more resources to demand reduction programs. The Drug Enforcement Administration, Los Angeles Police and the Los Angeles Sheriff's Office have been leaders in the development of demand reduction programs. As these programs have spread throughout the United States they have been acclaimed by educators and parents as very effective. These modest programs will not, in and of themselves, solve the drug problem but they do vividly point out that drug demand reduction efforts need to be greatly expanded, with more institutions directly involved in addressing the problem.

To claim that law enforcement supply reduction efforts have "failed" is also to deny the fact that arrests, seizures and forfeitures have significantly increased each year. The legalization argument does not address the issue of what the magnitude of the supply problem would be if no effort had been made. Considering the complex problems involved in supply reduction efforts, law enforcement would argue that our efforts have neither failed nor succeeded as well as we had hoped. Each year as we learn more about the problem, we make adjustments in our tactics and strategies. Each year, it becomes more difficult to smuggle all types of contraband into North America. Each year, it becomes more difficult to grow and conceal marijuana and tougher to transport the product from point to point. As we continue to improve our reduction efforts, seizures will continue to show modest increases. We would argue that we should stay the course on the supply reduction issue and not give in to a problem just because we have had only partial success.

Argument 4: Drug prohibition laws cause crime

Advocates of legalization argue that if we repealed laws presently making the production, distribution, purchase and consumption of drugs illegal, we would reduce the number of crimes. This is not only misleading but untrue. The issue is whether, as advocates claim, repeal would take the profit out of drug dealing and thus result in less drug-marketing violence. We believe the answer is no. Unless the legalization proponents intend to sell any drug, to any person, at any time, in any amount desired, a black market for drugs—and the attendant problems of crime and violence—will continue to exist. If drugs are freely available in the legal market and present addiction rates are maintained, it is reasonable to expect that the number of persons and the amount of drugs dispensed in the illegal market will increase. Thus, any short-term reduction of crime, however unlikely, would be rapidly negated. In the long term, the problems would probably be worse.

The argument that legalization would reduce the cost of drugs rests on the assumption that government can manufacture and distribute drugs more efficiently than the present illegal system, thus making drugs cheaper. Cheap drugs should, the argument states, reduce the necessity to commit crimes to finance drug purchases. Both of these assumptions are questionable. First, it is doubtful the government could compete against the present illegal system of distribution, particularly if the illegal system chose to compete with the government. The current cost of the production of a kilogram of cocaine is approximately $300. This amount of cocaine presently sells on the streets of Canada or the United States for anywhere from $15,000 to $30,000. Today, the price of cocaine is set by the cocaine cartel and is not subject to usual market forces. Firmly in control of supplies, enjoying a huge profit margin and not burdened by the bureaucracy that would be required by government market participation, the cartels would make competitive pricing by government difficult and might well require government subsidies—themselves a drain on economic resources—if implemented.

Furthermore, drug users not only have to buy drugs but also have the usual expenses of food and housing. Most heavy users are not able, or willing, to hold full-time employment after they pass a certain stage of addiction, yet they still need money. Since most addicts have found crime to be the easiest way to fund their lifestyles, it is reasonable to conclude that they will continue their predatory habits.

Finally, if the number of abusers increased as a result of legalization, then the amount of crime committed would also increase. Any reduction of violent crime achieved by the availability of inexpensive narcotics through government distribution would be negated by an increase in the number of drug users. The number of crimes such as assault, child abuse and violence committed routinely by drug users would tend to increase as the drugs became more readily available. This is a lesson we have learned from our experience with alcohol abuse. It need not be repeated.

Argument 5: High cost of law enforcement

Proponents of legalization estimate the cost of law enforcement in regard to the drug problem at about $10 billion annually, and suggest that this money could be better spent on drug rehabilitation programs. While $10 billion is a lot of money, it is only a tiny fraction of the funds spent annually to promote the public good. It is not even a great deal of money in comparison to private expenditures for personal comfort. In July 1988, as reported by CBS News, Americans spent $4.3 billion on electricity to run air conditioners. Put another way, the $10 billion amounts to $40 per year per person. When viewed in this context, the amount we spend on drug enforcement is modest. One other mitigating factor is the dollar value of seizures of assets from drug organizations. In 1987, for example, DEA seizures amounted to more than the agency's annual budget allocation.

The law enforcement community would certainly endorse building more drug treatment centers and is already working to build community support for such projects. Considering the gravity of the drug problem, the law enforcement community believes that an informed public would support allocation of funds to build adequate drug treatment centers without sacrificing our enforcement efforts. Since this is presently occurring throughout the United

States and Canada, it would tend to support our contention that the public is quite willing to help with drug treatment, without yielding on the illegality of drug use or the cost of law enforcement. Protection of the public by law enforcement is not in competition with drug education and treatment; these purposes are not a zero-sum game.

Argument 6: Legalization will not result in high drug use

Most proponents of legalization suggest that it would not lead to a dramatic rise in drug abuse. But even Nadelman suggested that this might be risky when he stated, "It is thus impossible to predict whether legalization would lead to greater levels of drug abuse, and exact costs comparable to most of alcohol and tobacco abuse."

Faced with the evidence of what has happened in terms of alcohol and tobacco abuse after sanctions were lifted on those substances, it is difficult to understand why it is impossible to predict the consequences of legalization of illicit drugs. Other historical examples show what happens when dangerous substances are not controlled. China's experience with opium from 1830 to 1930 is revealing. The Moslem Empire of the 11th century, the Inca Indians, Japan and Egypt all experienced significant drug dependency problems in their histories. The recent British attempt to control heroin abuse through the medical process has been a significant failure. We should also remember that morphine and cocaine were readily available in the form of patent medicines after the Civil War. The result was that America experienced a drug abuse problem similar in scope to what we see today. In general terms, most societies throughout history have had problems with drugs or drug abuse. Those societies that solved the problem did so in the same fashion we are trying today.

Relevant information can also be drawn from levels of abuse of currently legal drugs such as Valium. Our experience with methaqualone (Quaaludes), oxycondone (Percodan) and hydromorphone (Dilaudid) gives sufficient evidence that the control of legal drugs is difficult, expensive and not always successful. In each case, the drug has been widely abused, despite the prescription process. These substances have found their way into the black market, having been illegally diverted or manufactured. All these facts indicate that if presently illicit drugs were legalized, whether they were distributed by the private or the public sector under specific controls, people disposed to drug use would in fact use them. Generalized use could rise, and illegal means of meeting demand would continue.

Consideration must be given to the claim that illicit drugs are not, and would not, become as popular as tobacco and alcohol. This is a hazardous assumption. The most dangerous drugs might not become widely popular, but use of debilitating narcotics that adversely affect behavior could. The drug traffickers have shown themselves to be extremely shrewd at marketing strategies, and they will continue to promote demand. Much more important than legalization is the mobilizing of community pressure against illegal narcotics, as has been done with tobacco and alcohol.

Law enforcement officials do not predict that legalization would cause "doomsday." We argue that legalization promises no improvement and unnecessarily risks an increasing of drug abuse.

Argument 7: Illicit drugs are not as dangerous as believed

Legalization arguments depend on two additional assumptions: first, that illicit drugs are not as dangerous as is commonly believed and, second, that since some illicit drugs are highly dangerous, they are not likely to be popular. With respect to the first assumption, it is enough to say the medical community disagrees, as does every police officer who comes into contact with people debilitated by drugs from marijuana to "crack." The claim that illicit drugs are not dangerous falls of its own weight in the face of experience. The medical research community admits that current research is insufficient to say *exactly how dangerous* illicit drugs are to physical and mental health. Funding for additional medical research should be a high priority so that the full measure or risk can be grasped. For the present, we have enough information from emergency room and morgue records, accident statistics and overall costs of lost productivity from drug abuse to know that the dangers are real. As drug epidemics ebb and flow, and new substances are introduced into the marketplace, we tend to neglect such evidence. It was just a few years ago that cocaine was thought by many to be safe and non-addicting. The early studies of marijuana indicated some potential long-term health hazards, but most studies were done with samples containing half the THC now present in the sinsemilla and hydroponic varieties of marijuana. Current research tends to support the hypothesis that marijuana is a significant health hazard with a debilitating effect on motor skills. These are important skills used in driving, flying or handling a locomotive. Results of impairment have become all too familiar.

The claim that illicit drugs are not as dangerous as believed is wrong, and those who make it diminish the realism of the debate about legalization.

Conclusion

In our view, the proponents of legalization have not made a case for the freedom of individuals to choose to use illicit drugs regardless of the consequences. We believe the threat of intemperate drug use, whether legal or illegal, is a significant threat to our common welfare. The problem incurred by removing current sanctions would only make the threat more pronounced. We should protect ourselves by legislation where sanctions meet the combined test of common sense and the constitutions of the United States and Canada.

It is interesting to note that those making an argument for the legalization of illicit drugs have not recently made similar arguments on behalf of the common drunk. The drunk has become the "leper" in our society as a result of his behavior while intoxicated. The alcoholic is no longer considered in some quarters to be without responsibility for his conduct, but rather to be in violation of standards of common decency. Being drunk is not given any weight, in any quarter, as an excuse for violent or abusive behavior, and the drunk driver is being punished more severely than ever before in our history. Where are the defenders of the drunk? Where are the defenders of the smoker these days? Simply put, staunch defenders of the drunk and the smoker are gone because many have recognized that tolerance adversely affects the individual and the society. Laws have been strengthened and the sanctions of custom are being used to discourage consumption.

While some commentators would suggest that the problem of drug abuse is made worse by repressive measures of the criminal justice system, it is more reasonable to assume that the underlying cause of our problems lies within ourselves. Whether the causes reflect an absence of high personal standards, greed, inability to cope with rapid change or involuntary confinement to poverty, we must come to grips with the fact that a large number of people in our culture turn to drugs for relief. Law enforcement cannot address these basic problems alone. Considering the nature and the complexities of the underlying problems, it is obvious to us that the institutions of the family, education, religion, business, industry, media and government all have crucial stakes in the solution of the problem. Drug abuse is no longer the other fellow's problem.

Even though the problems of drug abuse are severe in both the United States and Canada, we should pause and consider the success we have had in reducing the number of people who are smoking cigarettes, and the steps that the Mothers Against Drunk Drivers (MADD), Students Against Drunk Driving (SADD) and Alcoholics Anonymous (AA) have taken to bring alcohol abuse problems under control. Some recent surveys indicate that our teenagers' drug use may have peaked and perhaps dropped a bit in recent years as a result of an effective demand reduction program. This is evidence that we have made significant progress in curbing the problem.

We need not haggle over how much each of us should do to bring the problem under control. We should not vilify those who suggest a different approach, or pass additional legislation in a hysterical atmosphere. This is a time to determine our best means and remedies for facing the problems and to move forthrightly to the task of reducing the problem to tolerable levels. For the short term, the law enforcement community hopes to continue to maintain reasonable and prudent pressure on supply interdiction and vigorous enforcement of existing laws, while at the same time continuing the development of demand reduction programs. This will buy time so that additional solutions can be developed and more players brought into the contest. In this regard, we in the law enforcement community stand ready to share our knowledge, resources and dedication to solving the problem with any institution, public or private, at any time.

We are sensitive to the fact that mistakes have been made in the attempt to control drug abuse. However, rather than dwell on finding a scapegoat, we really should be working together, as men and women of good faith, in an attempt to safeguard present and future generations. Controlling the problems of narcotics will take a long time, and it is not going to be as simple—or ostensibly as easy—as the mere legalization of drugs.

The authors wish to acknowledge the following individuals who gave freely of their ideas, command experience, and time to guide and direct this paper: Commander Robert C. Lamont, Metro-Dade P.D., Miami, Florida; Jacques Duchesneau, Montreal (Canada) P.D.; Lieutenant Leo Matrangolo, Baltimore County P.D., Towson, Maryland; Detective John Smith, Department of Public Safety, Pittsburgh, Pennsylvania; Division Chief C. Jerry Kennedy, Denver P.D.; Sergeant John Boulger, Minneapolis P.D.; Chief David Dotson, Office of Special Services, Los Angeles, California; Edwin Delattre, Bradley Fellow, Ethics & Public Policy Center, Washington, D.C.; Captain Bob Wilbur, Los Angeles County Sheriff's Department; Bob Berryman, Virginia State Police, Richmond, Virginia; Dr. Phyllis McDonald, International Association of Chiefs of Police, Arlington, Virginia; Robert Bryden, Director of Training, U.S. Drug Enforcement Administration, Quantico, Virginia.

PART 3

Toward Professional Police Standards

A New Perspective on Law Enforcement Policy

Phyllis P. McDonald

In recent years there has been a new emphasis on police manuals, policies, and procedures. Several reasons for this have been suggested. First, the relatively recent accreditation process probably has encouraged law enforcement executives to reassess their policies and procedures and to develop manuals that are complete and that reflect the best current thinking. Second, law enforcement executives have become increasingly professional. Third, and especially significant, the number and dollar amounts of civil liability suits are increasing, because citizens have become more knowledgeable about their civil rights and therefore have higher expectations of fair treatment by the police. Many cities are facing shrinking tax bases and other serious revenue problems and cannot afford the additional costs of judgments and settlements resulting from police management practices.

The impact of the review process

New police chiefs and sheriffs inevitably reach a stage when they realize that they need to review their agencies' policy manuals. This review process alone can have a significant impact on a law enforcement agency! It forces management to research industry standards to ensure that policies of the police agency are contemporary and represent the best thinking of the profession. Moreover, a thorough review and evaluation of current policies and procedures requires policy developers to look at their policies in light of current state and federal legislation, case law, local ordinances, and collective bargaining agreements. In short, any agency reassessing the state of its policies will apply both an industry standard and a legal or liability standard to its policies and procedures. Ultimately, as gaps are discovered, all essential policies will be included in the manual, and inadequate policies will be revised and updated.

The impact of an effective policy manual

A well-developed and sound policy manual can affect a law enforcement agency positively in many ways. First, the starting point of an effective policy manual is a statement of the agency's philosophy of policing, from which goals and objectives will be derived. Next, rules of conduct are clearly stated, followed by pertinent policies and procedures. The resulting document becomes a mechanism for management to communicate behavioral expectations to all ranks, particularly to officers and deputies on the street. If an unusual event is not covered by a policy or procedure in the manual, officers can use the philosophy, objectives, and rules of conduct as guides to decide how to proceed.

Second, a well-developed policy manual serves as an excellent training tool. Since both the substance and the specific procedures are presented clearly and in sequence, the training division can use the policy manual as a text for training both new recruits and in-service personnel.

Third, the policy manual must be regarded as a public documents. It is a source of information for officials of the jurisdiction about what services will be provided by police, how they will be provided, and why they, rather than other services, will be provided. In addition, citizens interested in the administration of law enforcement can have access to this document.

Finally, thoughtful and complete policy manuals play a most critical role in the courts. Some law enforcement personnel resist formulation of clear policies on grounds that they become standards to which officers may subsequently be held, but it is probable that these standards have a favorable impact on judge and jury. In the event of a civil suit, the police manual is the first step in demonstrating that a police agency is serious about defining appropriate and inappropriate behavior on the part of its officers.

Which policies does the agency need?

The size and content of police manuals vary widely. The smallest jurisdictions may have three-page manuals, whereas manuals of the largest agencies may require one-inch loose-leaf binders. An extensive range of issues and areas may be covered in a manual. Within this range, however, there is a core of high-risk issues that every agency should address; policies on other issues may be developed as needed. For example, every agency must have a policy on the use of force, but only an agency with a police chaplain's unit needs to have a related policy. Some agencies have not adopted the core policies.

Instead, policies have developed as a series of quick-fix responses to crises in the agency or the community or as reactions to legal decisions.

The most telling evidence of the process used to develop a policy manual is its table of contents. A table of contents that lists policies in chronological order almost certainly indicates that the manual has been developed largely in reaction to crises or to new laws that affect policing. Similarly, a table of contents that consists of individual topics such as off-duty employment, transfer policy, and handling of shoplifters, as opposed to groupings of policies into broader and more coherent headings (e.g., personnel, field procedures), indicates that the agency has not yet considered the universe of policies needed to properly do its job and to protect itself and its officers against liability. In these circumstances, instead of being prepared for predictable problems, the agency is always "behind the curve," developing a new policy after the fact each time a crisis or new situation arises—not sound insurance against liability suits. Consequently, officers make many decisions on the basis of intuition, what simply "feels right," or educated guesses about how related policies might be applied to the situation at hand.

How should an agency begin?

It is not difficult to develop a policy manual that covers all critical areas. The Commission on Accreditation for Law Enforcement Agencies has issued a complete review of the standards that each agency should have as a starting point.[1] An additional source of model policies is the National Law Enforcement Policy Center of the International Association of Chiefs of Police in Arlington, Virginia.

Agencies about to review their manuals for revision and updating should start with those policy areas that all professionals would consider "critical" or "high risk"—policy areas in which personal

---

National Law Enforcement Policy Center

Currently supported by a cooperative agreement between the International Association of Chiefs of Police and the U.S. Bureau of Justice Assistance, the National Law Enforcement Policy Center develops model policies on an ongoing basis and offers subscription to this service. Subscriptions entitle police agencies to have free research conducted into specific policy areas. For each model policy, the center publishes a "concepts and issues" paper to explain the intricacies of the policy so that executives can make informed decisions about which policies they want to implement.

injury, death, violation of rights, or civil suits may result if officers do not understand clearly what their departments expect of them. Examples of high-risk policy areas are: (1) use of force, both deadly and nonlethal; (2) hot pursuit; (3) powers of arrest; (4) search and seizure; and (5) handling of citizen complaints and discipline.

A 1986 report outlined areas in which departments had lost civil suits or settled out of court as shown in Table 1.[2]

It is interesting to note that more cities lost or settled cases involving allegations of excessive force (25.8 percent) than was the case of allegations of wrongful death. The policy areas that produce the largest number of civil rights suits are search and seizure and arrest procedures, such as field interrogations. At a minimum, if agencies review and update only the policies that control these behaviors, they will have taken a significant step toward professionalization. In their reviews of areas such as these, agencies should determine, first, whether they have relevant policies. If policies are in place, agencies should then consider whether the policies are adequate.

What should the agency do next?

Unfortunately, no police agency will be transformed by the simple act of writing policies. The following sections explain how to ensure that the policy manual will be used and how to integrate it with others systems in police agencies that support and reinforce adherence to policy manuals.

Components of the policy manual The foundation of a policy manual is a statement of philosophy prepared by the chief law enforcement executive. The chief executive has a major influence on the quality of both the work environment and the services rendered, and his or her statement of philosophy is the centerpiece of the department's administration. The policy manual should flow from this philosophy, and all procedures in the manual should be consistent with it.

It is especially important that chiefs or sheriffs state their own

Table 1. Police departments reporting suits lost or settled out of court.

Type of liability	Percentage of respondents
Excessive or wrongful use of force	25.8
Civil rights violations	22.0
Vehicle pursuit injuries	11.4
Employment discrimination	10.1
Wrongful death	5.8
Other	8.6

personal philosophies of policing or that they review existing philosophy statements to make certain that they are consistent with their own beliefs. A statement of philosophy that is meaningful to the chief ensures that his or her own behavior will remain consistent with the philosophy, and this consistency, or integrity, is central to support of the policy manual. The organizational development literature states that integrity, defined as consistency between beliefs and behavior, is critical to organizational success. For example, the chief or sheriff who claims to be a champion of participatory management but who continuously makes decisions on the basis of private advise from favored subordinates will cause employees to lose confidence in the department's leadership and in its command and administrative systems. Integrity on the part of the chief executive is the strongest possible reinforcement of adherence to the manual, because it demonstrates that the policy manual is taken seriously.

After the statement of philosophy has been developed, goals and objectives should be stated clearly. Then rules of conduct should be formulated. These rules should be absolute and should address only behaviors for which *right* actions can be clearly differentiated from *wrong* actions. Rules may deal with subjects such as corruption, abuse of alcohol or drugs, and other clearly inappropriate conduct.

These three components of the manual—philosophy, goals and objectives, and fundamental rules of conduct—set the tone of the agency and provide guidelines from which all succeeding policies and procedures should be derived.

Agency systems that support policy   The disciplinary system is a key reinforcer of the rules, policies, and procedures. A disciplinary system that is consistent, fair, and swift sends a secondary message that the policy manual is a document to be regarded with reverence. A rule that is relaxed for one subordinate because he or she has political contacts but that is firmly enforced for others makes a sham of the manual and the disciplinary system. A system that can be subverted and manipulated is no system at all.

Other systems, as well, support the policies in the policy manual. The training division that can, and does, regard the policy manual as a textbook for new recruits will ensure that training will contribute substantially to the quality of the agency's police service. Similarly, selection, promotion, and performance evaluation systems should be consistent with the philosophy of the law enforcement executive and should support the goals and objectives of the agency. The police department that claims to value positive interactions with citizens while it hires individuals who are hostile and aggressive or that measures performance primarily on the numbers of arrests made will polarize and confuse its officers.

Finally, the techniques used to develop, revise, or update a manual can contribute to its becoming a dynamic and viable document rather than one that gathers dust on officers' bookshelves. The developmental processes should provide for—and take seriously— the participation of the individuals who ultimately must implement and live with policy. There should be input from a wide range of staff as well as from professionals and citizens outside the agency. For example, in the formulation of a new policy on domestic violence, a small group composed of officers, community service providers, prosecutors, and judges can be assembled initially to brainstorm the components of the policy and reassembled later to review drafts of the policy. At whatever stage, review by those who will be affected by the policy is critical, for these reasons:

1. Those who will be affected by the policy will know best the specific needs in the policy area.
2. If the individuals affected by the policy already have some familiarity with it, they will be more likely to feel ownership in it once it is disseminated.

Conclusion

Law enforcement executives, city managers, and mayors should recognize that a policy manual is the *foundation* for quality police service. There may be times when a law enforcement executive may be tempted to promulgate a policy or change in procedure through word of mouth down through the chain of command. This process is risky, since one should not assume that the transmission will be accurate through each rank level. Therefore, should the executive attempt to institute a new policy via verbal transmission, he or she should also ensure that the written policy follows quickly. Verbal transmission of new policies or procedures should be regarded as a supplement to, not a replacement of, the written policy.

The policy manual is the accurate, memorialized, and complete statement of how police service will be conducted; it dictates quality, precision, and approach. This document is the formal expression of the chief's or sheriff's philosophy of policing and therefore represents an official statement and a commitment to the community.

1. *Standards for Law Enforcement Agencies* (Fairfax, VA: Commission on Accreditation for Law Enforcement Agencies, Inc., 1983). It is, of course, perfectly acceptable for agency manuals to include policies and procedures mandated by local conditions even though they are not found in the accreditation manual or other policy models.

2. James J. Fyfe, *Police Personnel Practices, 1986*, Baseline Data Reports, vol. 18, no. 6 (Washington, DC: International City Management Association, 1986), p. 10.

Establishing and Implementing Department Policies

Mark Kroeker and Candace S. McCoy

Police officers are human and they make human mistakes. Naturally, those mistakes are subject to critical review. The function of written department policies is to minimize the opportunity for error in critical situations.

Policy formulation must begin with a firm understanding of the emotional aspect of policing. People who want to become police officers are motivated partly by the variety and excitement of police work, and they become completely involved and committed to doing the job. But when an officer encounters a dangerous situation, he experiences a rush of adrenalin, which—in the absence of well-written policy—could result in improper actions.

A short anecdote illustrates this dynamic. An Indiana state police officer, responding to a call concerning a barricaded suspect, decided he was going to be a hero. He wanted to get the suspect out of that place all by himself. He forgot about asking for backup help; he forgot about other people. His adrenalin took over. As he approached the scene, he had his service revolver in one hand and a tear gas grenade in the other. Playing the hero, he pulled the grenade pin out with his teeth, approached the door and kicked it in, and *threw his gun* in with the suspect.

The officer stood there looking at the gas grenade in his hand, trying to figure out what to do. He waited for awhile and then peered around the corner, only to find that the barricaded suspect had committed suicide. The officer walked in, retrieved and holstered his weapon, and put the grenade pin back in the grenade.

This is a revision of an article originally published in the *Police Chief* magazine, vol. 55, no. 12, pages 34–41, 1988. Copyright held by The International Association of Chiefs of Police, 1110 N. Glebe Road, Suite 200, Arlington, Va. 22201, U.S.A. Further reproduction without express written permission from IACP is strictly prohibited.

He didn't tell that story for a long time, not wanting to publicize just *how* human he was. But, of course, all police officers are human beings, and when we are in a situation that heightens emotional response, we are fallible. The role of policy is to control that situation, to lower that heightened emotional response by preventing the events that lead up to it.

The Indiana officer in the example just mentioned, for instance, would not be placed in that same situation today. Those were the days before SWAT, before the officer was offered the many tactical choices that later became available to someone responding to such a call.

Sometimes controlling the events leading up to an otherwise explosive situation may simply mean taking advantage of available technology. One prime example of the type of police action that increases the flow of adrenalin is the auto chase. Using available technology can really help officers lower the heat in hot pursuit. And sometimes preventing tragic outcomes is simply a matter of faithfully using regulation equipment in the first place. A few years ago in Los Angeles, a young officer working by himself heard a description of a suspect for a robbery that had just been committed. The officer saw the suspect's car, radioed in, and pursued the fleeing suspect. The suspect lost control of his car and it jumped the sidewalk, wheels in the air, and plowed into the front window of a store. The police officer skidded in behind, jumped from the car, and the suspect came out from the broken glass inside the store with a loaded 9mm weapon in his hand. The officer took two or three rounds in the chest and subsequently died. The added tragedy of it is that his bullet-resistant vest was on his car seat.

Auto pursuits are high risk, high excitement activities, and the pursuit is the type of highly emotional event that can be controlled. A high speed chase is the example used throughout this article to illustrate the fact that policy can guide decisions and, therefore, prevent some tragedies.

At the end of the day, an officer who has successfully pursued and apprehended a suspect can say "Today I was in a pursuit and we got a guy wanted for a rape." The result is most important, but also the officer is pleased to have been directly and personally involved in an event that was exciting and consequential. Add to this personal satisfaction in direct involvement the demanding expectations of peers and teachers. At the police academy, recruits are told never to give up. "Go the extra mile, to the very end. If you're a quitter, you'll be a civilian quitter. And always help your partner. Support your partner; assist your partner." There are reports of Patton-type speeches by watch commanders who say, "If your partner is in a hospital bed, I'm going to be looking in the next bed for you. You better have gotten hurt trying to help him."

Against this organizational background and the normal reactions of human adrenalin, then, the department establishes formal policies designed to standardize the emotional event. Unfortunately, these policies often take no account of the emotional background of police work; or they are unclear, and are written in such a way that the police officer thinks they are designed to restrict him, not help him. They do not aid decision making—they confuse it. They are therefore often ignored, with the result that officers and their supervisors wind up in trouble with the courts and the media.

These problems can be substantially diminished, although not entirely eliminated, through careful policy formulation and implemention.

First of all, of course, there must be a written policy to govern critical events. Unwritten policies, though difficult to enforce, are still policies, and it is impossible to escape the consequences of bad policy making simply by pretending policy does not exist. A written policy should be part of the agency's description of its own work. Its tone must be congruent with the mindset of police officers. With auto pursuit policies, for instance, the mindset is: "Don't give up. Always pursue. Always help your partner." The written policy starts with that, and it says: "Don't give up. Always pursue, and you and your partner do it the smart way. And here are clear guidelines to do it right."

If the police officer's personal policy and the operational policy are the same, compliance is assured. But if the written language is in terms of "thou shall not, don't do this, never ever," then officers may to develop their own pursuit policies, because the formal pronouncements do not fit their perceptions of good police work.

If the policy must recognize the mindset of the individual police officer, the policy will be "Yes, pursue." So start there, and add guidelines.

Policies must be supportive in tone. When police trainers talk about officer survival, they say, "Here's something that will help you do your job a little bit better and protect yourself and the public." But when it comes to pursuit driving policy, the department issues a string of "don'ts." So the officers learn how to avoid rather than comply, and they also think about covering themselves. That's a recipe for trouble.

Clarifying policy

Writing policy is not easy. Despite several readings, some policies are still mystifying. How are street cops supposed to understand them?[1]

Departmental directives are often unclear. For some reason, although we speak clearly, we write obscurely. Good writing eliminates "fogginess" in police policies. There are two items in the "fog index": sentence length and word length.[2] To increase readability, write a shorter sentence and shorter words.

Consider auto pursuit policies. Their 60- and 70-word sentences are packed full of multi-cylinder words of four and five syllables. These policies will not communicate to the street cop. In fact, many police commanders will not understand them. So read your existing policies and try to rewrite them in a simpler form. Then circulate the draft and ask your colleagues to sign that they have read and understood it. If not, ask their suggestions for improvements.

Here is an example. The planning and research division of a large city police department had a legal information unit. Its personnel, some of whom were attorneys, were required to write training bulletins on legal issues. They were expected to take a case decision, explain what it meant, and then send it to the officers to direct their behavior. The commanding officer of the unit received one of these bulletins, read it, and didn't understand it. He called the legal information unit and recommended that the draft be circulated to two or three officers in each of two or three divisions to ascertain their understanding and get their suggestions. They did that. When the document came back, it had been completely rewritten. The new version was clear; everybody understood it.

This writing method might take more time and energy, but it is superior to other more formal but less informed policy formulation procedures. It is a small field test of the policy before it goes into effect; it produces clear directives, and it allows several people to contribute to the final policy.

A final point on clarity: this is the age of the half-read page. If the policy is too long, few officers will read the entire document. Put the most important points first. Tell those officers, when they first pick it up, the reason for its importance. Then tell them the decision factors that will help them achieve that important goal.

Developing decision-making skills

The key—the essential ingredient both in policy and in training—is the decision factor. Pursuit driving, use of force, or any of a number of other high-adrenalin and high-visibility tasks hinge on the effectiveness of decision-making. Is that officer on the street making a valid choice? Thus, we must train officers in decision-making skills.

"Your policy is only as good as your training in it." That is very accurate, though it should be amended to reflect the fact that humans can be *developed* rather than merely trained. People have the capacity to learn, to adapt and to think about what is being done. Although police departments use the word "training," it is more precise to think in terms of human development. Police departments have to develop in the officer the capacity to think carefully, to ward off that adrenalin rush. When an officer confronts a crisis on the street, that officer should have developed the ability to sort out the options and determine the best method for handling the situation. With proper development, the officer will not consider an emotional response to be the best method.

There are various means of developing decision-making skills. Obviously, the best is on-the-job training. Actually being exposed to the trauma and many important decision factors of an auto pursuit, for instance, will impress those factors upon the thinking of any recruit driver. But this method is costly. The actual scenarios are infrequent, sporadic. Immediate feedback from more experienced officers is often absent. And if the recruit makes a mistake, as any learner often will, it is a real-world mistake and people may be hurt.

Simulation might not be perfect, but it is the more realistic solution. On LAPD's driving course, for instance, the officer is placed behind the wheel and given as much stimulation as possible to apply emotional pressure. The recruit spends 24 hours behind the wheel and another six hours in the classroom. The classroom matches up the pursuit policy with the experience in simulated driving. What decisions did you make along the way? What were the outcomes? What alternatives were available? Do you see why the policy prefers one alternative over another?

Simulation is expensive, but the loss of life that would occur without it is worse. Simulation gives the officer the actual feeling of being there, after which pivotal decisions are reviewed and critiqued. During the simulation, there are some sweaty palms and then sighs of relief. And if the driver crashes and "kills" three people, they are not real people, and the student knows not to make those decisions again in the real world.

The LAPD pursuit driving course is at a local fairground, and of course it is just not the same as going 80 mph on Crenshaw Boulevard with a red light ahead and all the traffic jammed. But some simulation is better than none, and new technology can even simulate the busiest intersection and the most unusual chase factors in your city. This equipment may be too expensive for one agency to buy, but perhaps it could be obtained on a regional share basis.

Applying technology

Decisions are choices made from two or more alternatives. One thing police administrators can do for officers is to define the alternatives and show why some are better than others. That is the task of policy and training. Next, it is important to equip the officer with adequate means to act on a decision once it is made. Technology can make a difference.

Regarding technology, many organizations apply restrictions before carefully thinking about what the technology can do. For example, we say "that will never work," or "that's unconstitutional," or "that will get thrown out in court," not because these things are true, but because we do not want to think creatively. Weighing new technologies and programs is hard work, and sometimes it is easier to make excuses based on supposedly powerful outside pressures than to think through the possibilities.

Thinking in a very broad and open way about what we can do technologically to help officers make good decisions and carry them out is a continuing task for the police manager. Important legal, moral, and ethical constraints are always present, but we should first think creatively about the possibilities, and then address the problems.

An ominous-sounding but useful example is the "death ray." The technology is available today to deenergize the electrical system of a car in motion. An officer could direct the ray at a fleeing suspect's car, and the effect would be the same as if the brakes were slowly applied. There were 842 pursuits in Los Angeles last year, and the officers who initiated them had to make some very difficult decisions about whether it was appropriate to endanger their lives and the lives of innocent bystanders in order to pursue. This ray device could substantially reduce the number of pursuits, and any officer who had it available would certainly have an easier time making decisions than officers do now.

Of course, this will not solve all problems. Suspects could probably jump from stolen cars that had been deactivated and officers would have to catch them some other way. But at least the police would recover the car intact, without flying down the street endangering their own lives and those of bystanders. These devices that override electrical systems can be installed in cars by manufacturers; police would then use a device like a garage door opener to activate them. Would this violate the Fourth Amendment? It may or may not, depending on how the technology is used, what it can do, and how it can be controlled. Find answers to those questions, and then match the answers to the legal issues.

Finally, leaders cannot formulate policy without data, and they cannot implement policy without supervision. In the writing stage and then the training/development stage of policy making, decision factors are the critical points of analysis. One way to understand those factors and to guide officers in their choices is to gather information about actual officer performance on the street. Good statistical systems capture this information, and it is powerful. Otherwise, citizens fall prey to news media hype, to dramatic stories and police reaction to them. These stories may be completely atypical, but nobody can prove that without good information describing normal events.

In pursuits, for instance, data collection should include how many pursuits were conducted and under what conditions, who was pursued, how the chase was resolved, and the length of the pursuit. If the information system can answer these questions, police can operate from a historical rather than a hysterical perspective. If those statistics are good, they can demonstrate the operation of the overall policy to courts and municipal policymakers, and not fixate on the one unusual, tragic event.

Supervision is also systematic. Most problems are a result of poor supervision and weak command. These deficiencies arise from knee-jerk reactions to crises. Policy lurches around, responding to a series of unfortunate incidents, instead of being a systematic approach to predictable and preventable problems. A solid control system can be built from the bottom up, with good review and participation throughout the organization. The best system of supervision and policy development includes the police officer, the supervisor, the training reviews and the command reviews.

Implementation of the suggestions offered here will not prevent all problems, but in the long run they might diminish their impact. Knowledgeable, clear-headed decision making is critical to daily police work. Police managers who want to encourage good decisions by field officers can begin by making logical, clear choices themselves in departmental policies, training and development, and technical support.

1. A study of police job stress conducted by Dr. Peter Gregg, San Diego Regional Training Center, reported that police officers rated "unclear management orders, directives, and policies" as their fourth most critical job stressor. The first was being shot or shot at; the second was having your partner shot or shot at; and the third was being called to the scene of an emergency with little information.

2. The "fog index" is a device for determining how many years of education are required to understand a document. For example, if an essay were rated at 8 or 9, that indicates that a person with an eighth or ninth grade education could understand it. *Readers' Digest* has a fog index of 8, *Time* magazine is rated 10, the *Wall Street Journal* is 11, the California Penal Code is 26, and the Bible has a fog index rating of 6 or 7. One police policy statement was analyzed and given a fog index of 33. Apparently, an officer would have to be working on a third Ph.D. to begin to understand this policy. Field officers should not have to develop that degree of reading comprehension to understand what their department is directing them to do.

Controlling
Police Vehicle
Pursuits

James J. Fyfe

By now, nearly every scholar or practitioner who has studied or commented upon police vehicle pursuit policy and practice has recommended that the duty to apprehend fleeing motorists take a back seat to the police obligation to protect life and property.[1] Because vehicle pursuits are so dangerous and because officers are likely to act rashly in the heat of the moment, the literature generally agrees that the decisions of officers faced with potential pursuits must be guided by clear administrative policy and extensive training.

This perspective is nothing new. In 1971, former Santa Ana (California) official Thomas F. Adams wrote that

protection of life and property still applies to the high-speed chase, and it includes the lives and property of the individual being pursued, the officer and any innocent people who might become involved in a traffic collision as a direct result of the chase. At some time during the chase, it may be necessary to abandon the chase to uphold this police responsibility.[2]

Further, the data available to former Los Angeles police official N. F. Iannone in 1974 led him to the conclusion that officers' authority to engage in high-speed pursuits should be carefully limited. He noted that as many as 500,000 hot pursuit incidents occur in the U.S. each year, with 6,000 to 8,000 ending in crashes causing injury or death. He went on to point out that over 90 percent of these chases begin with traffic violations. Over half the incidents involve alcohol; many involve male drivers under age twenty-four, and over half the apprehended offenders have had one or more licenses suspended or revoked in the past. Pursuits are most likely at night and over weekends, and relatively few involve stolen cars.[3]

In 1976, another Californian, former Berkeley police officer

Gwynne Peirson, advised officers to think carefully for themselves about whether the risks of a chase are worth taking, particularly if it involves a minor violation, if it is in a densely populated area, or if there is another means of apprehension. Peirson went on to say:

> While some officers rationalize that in certain instances, and in the interest of public safety, a wanted person must be apprehended at any cost, the officer making the decision as to whether the risk is justified should apply the same standard in weighing the alternatives as he would in deciding whether to fire his revolver in a situation where innocent bystanders would be endangered. Additionally, a logical argument can be made that a high-speed chase involves more risks than shooting at a fleeing suspect. Whenever the officer fires his revolver, the primary risk is that he may accidentally strike a bystander. By comparison, in a high-speed chase, the officer not only has his own actions to be concerned with, but he must also consider the possibility that he will cause other cars to have accidents in attempting to get out of the way, and that chasing the suspect may force that auto to have an accident that will kill or injure innocent parties.[4]

The data

The findings of studies undertaken since Adams, Iannone, and Peirson set pen to paper underscore the great danger of vehicle pursuits. In 1983, the California Highway Patrol (CHP) studied 683 vehicle pursuits involving both its officers and the members of ten municipal departments.[5] Four years later, sociologist Geoffrey Alpert published a study of 398 pursuits by officers of the Metro-Dade (Florida) Police Department. Even taking into account the likelihood that the CHP pursuits more frequently occurred on open highways than was true of the chases Alpert studied, the data collected and analyzed in these studies indicate that pursuits in California and Dade County came to remarkably similar ends. Table 1 shows that about one-third of the chases in both California and Dade ended in accidents (29% and 33%, respectively), and that one-eighth resulted in injuries (11% in California; 14% in Dade). In both places, 1 percent resulted in deaths, and a great number of fleeing motorists escaped apprehension (23% in California; 37% in Dade County).

These percentages, however, are based on numbers that include pursuits voluntarily terminated by police (4% in California; 7% in Dade) or by motorists (36% in California; 18% in Dade). It is not possible to determine how many—or whether—such cases also resulted in other negative outcomes (e.g., a fender-bender, followed by voluntary termination), but it is probable that many voluntary terminations occurred without other incident. If such cases could be identified and subtracted from the total, the percentage of negative outcomes (among cases in which officers or motorists persisted in

Table 1. Vehicle pursuit outcomes in California and Dade County, Florida.

Pursuit outcome	California Highway Patrol (n=683)[1]	Metro-Dade Police Department (n=398)[2]
Accident	29%	33%
Injury	11%	14%
Death	1%	1%
Escape	23%	37%
Voluntarily terminated by police	4%	7%
Voluntarily terminated by motorist	36%	18%

[1]Source: California Highway Patrol, *Pursuit Study* (Sacramento: California Highway Patrol, 1983).
[2]Source: Geoffrey P. Alpert, "Questioning Police Pursuits in Urban Areas," *Journal of Police Science and Administration* 15 (1987): 298-306.

pursuit) would increase accordingly, and we would have a better picture of the costs of pursuits that continue until one or the other party is forced to stop.[6] In more simple language, the California and Dade studies did not sort out cases in which somebody ran out of nerve before disaster struck. Consequently, these studies do not tell us the cost of pursuits in which either party gives up in the interests of safety.

Interpreting the data
Where the CHP and Alpert studies do differ greatly is on interpretation of their similar findings. Alpert generally encouraged police to great caution and to further study designed to assure the relevance of policy and training.[7] The CHP report, however, concluded by recommending that officers be given what is essentially a blank check in pursuit situations. To wit: "Undoubtedly, innocent people may be injured or killed because an officer chooses to pursue a suspect, but this risk is necessary to avoid the even greater loss that would occur if law enforcement agencies were not allowed to aggressively pursue violators."[8]

Thus, CHP concluded that the long-term police obligation to protect lives and to prevent anarchy on the highways outweighed the more immediate dangers of "aggressive" pursuits. This conclusion is based on the premise that great numbers of motorists would flee the police if officers' authority to engage in high-speed pursuit were curtailed. In fact, there is little in CHP's data or in other studies to support such a premise or to suggest that motorists may be aware of police pursuit policies.[9] Despite the consensus for restraint among authorities other than the CHP researchers, court records and newspaper stories describe many tragedies that suggest that CHP's conclusion closely parallels the practices of many police agencies. Consider the following in the light of the calls for restraint by Adams, Iannone, Peirson, and others:

A young woman en route home from her bridal shower was killed when her car was broadsided by a suburban police officer who had sped through a red light in pursuit of a traffic violator. Television news viewers that night were treated to shots of a highway littered with shower gifts and auto parts.

Police saw a speeding motorcycle on a highway in a major city. Moments later, the motorcyclist and his young female passenger were fatally injured in a fiery head-on collision with a police car that had joined the chase. In the suit that followed, one of the pursuing officers testified that he had driven as fast as 143 miles per hour to apprehend traffic violators.

In the parking lot of a rural fast-food restaurant, teenage boys riding in a pick-up truck whistled at some teenage girls. Police signalled the driver to stop but, apparently afraid of being caught breaking his father's prohibition on beer in the truck, the driver fled. He and three of his friends died a few minutes later when he lost control of the truck on a winding country road and drove into a boulder.

The bride-to-be, the motorcyclist's passenger, and the kids in the back of the pick-up truck had no say in their fates. They died because others made stupid choices—to flee—and because police officers chose, literally, to pursue them at any cost. Yet, and despite what their formal policies may have stated, none of the police departments involved in these incidents were critical of the actions of the officers involved. Instead, the officers' actions were approved and defended in court by their departments and their departments' lawyers. (See the accompanying sidebar for an example.)

Addressing emotions and values in pursuit policy

To understand why is there so much difference between what most police authorities say and what some police agencies do, one must look at the emotions that surround vehicle pursuits. These emotions arise from the fact that motorists who refuse to stop give officers what are, in effect, unexpected slaps in the face.

Drivers generally are deferential to police officers. When patrol cars pull onto highways, motorists check speedometers, slow to the speed limit, and usually do not call attention to themselves by pass-

Vehicle pursuits: an example

Perhaps the most spectacular chase defended by a police agency occurred in 1984. On a Saturday night, two young men met two young women at a cocktail lounge. At eleven o'clock, all four left in a seven-year-old Cadillac driven by one of the young men. Almost immediately, two officers saw that the Cadillac's headlights were out and signalled the car to a stop. The young man driving the car accelerated and led the police on a high-speed chase.

Over winding roads with speed limits between 25 and 35 miles per hour, the chase covered five miles in five minutes, an average of about 60 miles per hour. Then, according to police reports, the Cadillac struck a Pontiac Phoenix that was coming from the opposite direction and making a left-hand turn. The collision knocked the Pontiac's engine into its passenger compartment, trapping its driver and passenger.

The Cadillac then became airborne, rotating and turning over as it flew. Upside down and more than six feet in the air, it struck the wall of a house at a point 112 feet from the collision with the Pontiac. It then bounced off the house and, 138 feet from the initial impact point, struck a telephone pole, snapping it nine and a half feet above the ground. The impact tore the entire left side off the car and threw the driver and his front seat passenger out of the vehicle.

The Cadillac then came to the ground 155 feet from the point of initial impact. Rotating on its roof, it skidded another 70 feet until it struck an Oldsmobile travelling in the opposite direction. It then bounced off the Oldsmobile and finally came to rest 264 feet from the spot at which it had struck the Pontiac. By then its roof had virtually disintegrated.

The crash killed the driver of the Cadillac (who had a blood alcohol reading of 0.13) and the young woman who shared the front seat. His two rear seat passengers and the driver of the Pontiac survived with serious injuries.

ing police cars. When police attempt to stop motorists, the vast majority of drivers pull immediately to the curb. When they come face-to-face with the officers who have stopped them, most motorists are polite, respectful, and apologetic. During a project on violence reduction, for example, in-car observers watched Metro-Dade police officers initiate 1,051 stops of traffic violators. Only 10 motorists—fewer than one in 100—attempted to flee. Only 27—about one in 40—were disrespectful or otherwise gave officers what could be considered a "hard time."[10]

Police officers, accustomed to dealing with citizens who accede to their wishes and directives, often take motorists' flight as the ultimate sign of disrespect, and are likely to react out of anger and

The police investigator who reconstructed the accident placed part of the blame for it on the driver of the Pontiac. In his view, the Pontiac driver "had ample time and sight distance to take appropriate evasive action, even if [the unlit Cadillac] was travelling at a speed in excess of 90 miles per hour." Although uninvolved witnesses placed the officers close behind the Cadillac at the time of the collision, the investigator's report also concluded that the officers never exceeded 55 miles per hour and were a mile or more from the collision. The investigator's superiors agreed and, in the end, ruled that this chase was reasonable, as did a jury who heard a suit brought by the driver of the Pontiac.

The police chief of the city in which this accident occurred would probably not share this view. Had his officers been notified of this chase prior to its spectacular conclusion, they would have been governed by the following pursuit policy:

"Effective immediately, the Officer-in-Charge of each shift will be solely responsible for the decision of whether to commence or continue a high speed chase.

"The concept of these so-called 'high-speed chases' becomes more and more dangerous and ridiculous when the object of the pursuit is to resolve some minor motor vehicle violation.

"Too many people have been killed or seriously injured as a result of some of these incidents. Consequently, unless the object of the pursuit has committed (not suspected of) a serious offense, i.e., murder, rape, robbery, etc., a high speed chase will not be tolerated. If necessary to pursue, it must be done with the utmost caution. If it appears inevitable that a death or serious injury will result from a chase, stop the pursuit. We have many other methods of apprehension at our disposal.

"This order is effective immediately and the Officer-in-Charge of each shift shall be held accountable for its enforcement."

sudden rushes of adrenalin, rather than on the basis of logic and professional responsibility. When this happens, the motorist's flight becomes a personal challenge, and officers may risk themselves, those they pursue, and uninvolved motorists and pedestrians during reckless pursuits of people who turn out to be nothing more than panic stricken young traffic violators.

Before getting to the substance of pursuit policy, therefore, police officials should make certain that they recognize that the mere fact of a motorist's flight is likely to encourage officers to disregard everything they have been taught. Officials should also make certain that officers are given clear notice that violations of policy will not subsequently be excused as understandable responses to extreme provocations. Indeed, police pursuit policies exist for no other reasons than to influence officers' decisions and behavior under extreme provocations, and such policies mean nothing if officers do not understand that they will be enforced.

One way to assure that police behavior at potential pursuits is only minimally affected by emotions is to limit officers' discretion in these heat-of-the-moment situations. At the extreme, this can be accomplished by prohibiting officers from pursuing at all. As in virtually all police operational areas, however, policies and rules that allow for no exception generally prove to be unworkable. Instead, it is probably advisable to shift as many decisions as possible out of the cars directly involved in pursuits.

Training, for example, should prepare officers for the adrenalin rush they are likely to experience when motorists flee. Then, like defensive driving courses that prepare officers to react to sudden and unexpected skids, training should clearly define the response that is most likely to produce the most desirable outcome. In this way, officers will have decided what to do in pursuit situations *before* they actually occur.

In addition, policy should clearly assign supervisors and radio dispatchers the authority and responsibility to discontinue chases when it becomes clear that the dangers of continued pursuit outweigh the benefits of apprehension. Doing this, of course, requires that police agencies define *desired outcomes* and that they conduct cost-benefit analyses of pursuits. Here, as in every sphere of police activity, there should be no doubt that the most desirable outcome to a police pursuit is the one that best meets the police responsibility for the immediate protection of life and property.

Training and policy should also stress that officers' personal driving skills and the capabilities of police vehicles are only secondary considerations in weighing the costs and benefits of specific pursuits. As Alpert notes, police cars were involved in only a only a small percentage of the accidents that terminated pursuits in the cases he studied. Instead, most accidents involved pursued vehicles and other uninvolved motorists or pedestrians.[11]

Logic suggests the reasons for this finding, and logic also suggests that this finding should lead to a presumption in favor of not pursuing. When pursuits begin, they involve two parties. The first party is usually a well-trained, well-rested, and physically fit police officer strapped into a heavy duty and/or high performance police vehicle. Thus, such officers rightly assume, if anybody can drive safely on public roads at high speeds, it is they.

As Iannone's earlier comments suggest, however, the second party is often a young man whose recklessness and irrational courage have been inflated by liquor, drugs, or fear of being caught in Dad's car without permission. Often he is inexperienced and unlicensed or, as in the case of the motorcyclist described above, has already lost a driver's license for dangerous or incompetent driving. In other words, he often reacts to the officer's signalling without thinking, without realizing his own limits, and without considering the welfare of those around him. Worse, as a pursuit continues and as the reality of what he has done sets in, he is likely to become increasingly rattled, desperate, and dangerous.

When this happens and the chase is underway, it no longer involves only two parties and their passengers. It involves innocent users of the street who are not tuned to police radio bands, who have no notice that they may be in the paths of pursuits proceeding at breakneck speeds, and who have no training as to what to do when they are surprised by cars traveling at speeds that exceed posted limits by a factor of two or three. At this point, well-trained and well-equipped police officers who know what is going on are probably in less danger than anybody else on the roads on which pursuits occur. In this sense, police should not choose to continue pursuits merely because they feel little personal danger. Instead, they should base their choices on the danger pursuits present to others.

Specific pursuit policy components

Laying back   Dog race aficionados know that the faster the greyhounds run, the faster the mechanical rabbit must travel in order to keep them coming. So it is with vehicle pursuits: as fleeing motorists are more hotly pressed, they increase their speeds—and the dangers they present—in order to stay ahead of the police.

Thus, once officers have decided that a situation is serious enough to void the presumption against pursuit, they should merely attempt to keep the violating vehicle in sight, until it is inevitably forced to stop by some traffic condition (e.g., traffic stopped at a red signal light). If, at any time, it becomes impossible to accomplish even this without causing undue danger to life and property, officers should break off pursuit: one simply does not risk lives in order to issue traffic tickets.

Overtaking   Forcing vehicles off the road or attempting to force them to a stop by passing them exposes citizens and officers to so much risk that it is difficult to conceive of any situation in which such actions would be justified. These actions should not be permitted except in the most extreme situations and with supervisory approval.

Roadblocks   The literature is also in agreement that establishment of roadblocks to stop fleeing vehicles should be undertaken only in the most extreme circumstances.[12] While roadblocks may seem to be the least aggressive means of stopping fleeing vehicles, they are extremely dangerous. Those in flight may be unable to avoid hitting them or, in attempting to pass around them, may be unable to stop without hitting other obstacles. When roadblocks are used, they should be extremely well-lit and positioned in places where fleeing subjects have much opprtunity to see them at a distance. By not blocking off entire roadways, roadblocks should be symbolic attempts to intimidate motorists to stop, rather than impassable barriers designed to force those in flight to stop or crash.

Conclusions

The relevant literature generally indicates that high-speed pursuits are extremely dangerous operations in which suspects and officers are likely to act irrationally and to become involved in hazardous skills contests. It also indicates that these situations most often involve minor violators, that their irrationality is frequently explained by the fact that they are drunk—and thus especially dangerous—and that the officers' actions at these situations should be guided by careful training and supervision. It is simply not adequate to leave to officers' "good sense" decisions as to how to handle potential high-speed pursuits, because experience has shown that officers are likely to operate under influences other than "good sense" at these times. An integral component of such supervision is a clearly articulated departmental policy on high-speed pursuit, and the agency that does not have and abide by such a policy is simply not doing all it should to protect lives and property.

1. See Thomas F. Adams, *Police Field Operations* (Englewood Cliffs, NJ: Prentice-Hall, 1985); Thomas F. Adams, *Police Patrol Tactics and Techniques* (Englewood Cliffs, NJ: Prentice-Hall, 1971), p. 239; Geoffrey P. Alpert, "Questioning Police Pursuits in Urban Areas," *Journal of Police Science and Administration* 15 (1987): 298-306; Geoffrey P. Alpert and Patrick Anderson, "The Most Deadly Force: Police Pursuits," *Justice Quarterly* 3 (1986): 1-13; Center for the Environment and Man, Inc., *A Study of the Problem of Hot Pursuits by the Police* (Washington, DC: U.S. Department of Transportation, 1970); Commission on Accreditation for Law Enforcement Agencies, Inc., *Standards for Law Enforcement Agencies* (Fairfax, VA: CALEA, 1985), Standard 41.2.8; N. F. Iannone, *Principles of Police Patrol* (New York: McGraw-Hill, 1974), pp. 200-210; Gwynne Peirson, *Police Operations* (Chicago: Nelson-Hall, 1976), pp. 75-77.

2. Adams, *Police Patrol Tactics and Techniques*, p. 239.

3. Iannone, *Principles of Police Patrol*, pp. 200-202.

4. Peirson, *Police Operations*, pp. 75-77.

5. California Highway Patrol, *Pursuit Study* (Sacramento: California Highway Patrol, 1983).

6. Some hint of the extent of this understatement is provided by Alpert, "Questioning Police Pursuits in Urban Areas," which indicates that accidents ended 54 percent of the pursuits that resulted in apprehension.

7. *Ibid.*

8. California Highway Patrol, *Pursuit Study*, p. 21.

9. Indeed, after involvement as a consultant and expert witness in several civil cases emanating from police-pursuit-related accidents, the evidence convinces me that the reverse is true in most American jurisdictions. Jurors (who are hard put to conceive of any justification for running from the police) typically have little sympathy for motorists who flee the police or for innocent victims of such pursuits. Instead, jurors typically expect the police to do anything necessary to apprehend those who flee in vehicles and, perhaps influenced by the exploits of movie and TV cops, jurors regard citizens killed or injured in such chases as unfortunate victims of the luck of the draw.

10. James J. Fyfe, *The Metro-Dade Police/Citizen Violence Reduction Project: Final Report*, vol. 2 (Washington, DC: Police Foundation, 1988), pp. K-22, K-52.

11. Alpert, "Questioning Police Pursuits in Urban Areas," p. 305.

12. Adams, *Police Field Operations*, p. 66.

The Accreditation Process

Cornelius J. Behan

Virtually every aspect of human endeavor has advanced dramatically in the twentieth century, and law enforcement is no exception. In technology, policing has come from the Bertillon identification system, through genetic research, to DNA comparisons; computers are replacing manual files and paper messages; foot patrols are bolstered by radio cars, aircraft, and community policing; countless lives have been saved through hostage negotiations that have replaced the traditional method of violent confrontation. To this impressive list should be added a new concept that will take American policing into the next century and beyond—law enforcement accreditation.

Although accreditation is not new, its application to law enforcement is. In the past forty years, in addition to the advances already mentioned, thousands of police officials have earned college and postgraduate degrees. Spurred by funding from the 1968 Omnibus Crime Control and Safe Streets Act and by their own motivations, police personnel have flocked to colleges and universities. Criminal justice curricula, intertwined with the regular academic offerings and adjusted to accommodate shift work, have appeared across the country. Inquiry, research, and experimentation have become an obsession, as new thinking has brought social scientists and police practitioners together. The "newest breed" is demanding excellence of themselves and their departments. Recruitment of minorities and women has made the mixture richer, setting the stage for further healthy change. Among the most important changes is the development and acceptance of the idea of accrediting police departments.

The evolution of law enforcement accreditation

The concept of accreditation originated with the adoption of standards for institutions of higher learning, including medical schools, and soon spread to hospitals. Its application to police agencies can be traced to 1929, when President Hoover formed the Wickersham Commission to study crime and the justice system. The commission's report on law enforcement administration and operations identified many weaknesses and recommended many improvements.[1] Because of the commission's influence and prestige, the report gave real form to the idea of standards for law enforcement.

Prominent authors, including August Vollmer in 1936[2] and O. W. Wilson in 1950,[3] emphasized the need for some degree of consistency and provided the publications and scholarly foundation from which many standards have been developed. Meanwhile, the positive effects of the fire rating system on the fire service and of the old National Safety Council ratings on traffic enforcement fueled interest.

In 1967 another presidential body was named—the President's Commission on Law Enforcement and Administration of Justice. Its reports identified policing problems and proposed solutions in many areas, and it, too, was influential.[4] About the same time, the federal Office of Law Enforcement Assistance, the forerunner of the Law Enforcement Assistance Administration (LEAA), was established, and in 1968 Congress passed the massive Omnibus Crime Control and Safe Streets Act.

LEAA pushed the development of standards by creating the National Advisory Commission on Criminal Justice Standards and Goals (NAC), which published an extensive set of standards in 1973.[5] The legal profession also saw the need to establish levels of performance in law enforcement: in 1973 the American Bar Association (ABA) published standards,[6] which, along with the NAC standards, served as a valuable resource in the later development of the accreditation standards. In 1974 another model for law enforcement standards and accreditation was initiated when federal funds were granted to the American Correctional Association to refine its standards[7] and to develop an accreditation process.

For years, of course, the courts also played a role in setting standards for police. Police practices that the courts found offensive or unconstitutional led to decisions restricting police methods and procedures. Although these decisions were mostly negative directions *not* to engage in specific activities, they also provided de facto performance measurements against which police operations could be compared.

Many people in law enforcement were well aware of the shortcomings in police practice. Regardless of the merits of the early attempts to establish police standards, however, police leaders knew that standards set by organizations with different agendas would not take root. In the view of many, it was impossible for organizations outside policing—the courts and the ABA, for example—to understand and take the police perspective, and no one law enforcement organization could provide the industrywide perspective required for true improvement. What was needed to develop realistic performance standards for police work, these leaders reasoned, was a meeting of the minds that, through debate and negotiation, would develop a professional consensus about the appropriate state and direction of American policing.

Consequently, a newly created consortium of four national police organizations petitioned LEAA, which was soon to go out of business, for a $5 million grant to develop law enforcement standards. Almost as its last gasp, LEAA provided these funds, and a long-time dream of many police professionals was about to come true.

The members of the new consortium were the International Association of Chiefs of Police (IACP), the National Sheriffs' Association (NSA), the National Organization of Black Law Enforcement Executives (NOBLE), and the Police Executive Research Forum (PERF). These four organizations represented approximately 80 percent of American law enforcement agencies, clear evidence that support for accreditation ran wide and deep in the police community.

In September 1979, the Commission on Accreditation for Law Enforcement Agencies, Inc. (CALEA) was formed. The twenty-one original members were unanimously agreed upon by the four founding organizations, a requirement that holds true today. Commission seats were allotted to eleven law enforcement professionals and ten leaders in the public and private sectors. In 1980, CALEA was incorporated as an independent, nonprofit organization.

The commission immediately began work on developing *measurable* standards aimed specifically at (1) delivery of law enforcement services; (2) increasing citizen and officer confidence in law enforcement standards and practices; and (3) effecting greater standardization of police administrative and operational practices.

Over the next four years, the program evolved through continuous testing and refining of the standards and assessment processes, including reviews of standards by representative individuals and field testing by 350 law enforcement agencies of varying types and sizes. In the end, 944 standards were adopted.

What had seemed to be an impossible task was now complete. Measurable standards tailored to all types and sizes of police departments were a reality. The commission did not dictate how the standards were to be met and, in essence, limited itself to identifying administrative and operational areas that should be addressed through departmental policies and procedures tailored to the needs of individual jurisdictions. In other words, the standards generally did not tell police departments *what* their manuals should say about specific issues. Instead, the standards told police departments *what issues* they should say something *about* in their manuals.[8]

Preparing for accreditation

When a department is considering accreditation, the timing is important. Agencies undergoing significant restructuring, leadership change, major internal investigations, significant litigation, or labor unrest should seriously consider postponing the accreditation process. Also, an unstable political climate may suggest postponement, especially since the unqualified, uninterrupted support of the elected officials is crucial.

Commitment Accreditation begins with the commitment of the agency's chief executive. There is no place for lip service or for merely cutting an order and expecting accreditation to fall into place. The chief must get staff and employees, as well as officials and administrators, to buy into the process and must use every opportunity to sell accreditation to the agency's personnel, to the rest of local government, to the private sector, and to the community at large.

Particularly important is a commitment from the top elected official and the chief administrative officer or city/county manager. Involvement and commitment at all levels within an agency are obviously important, but a chief who cannot obtain strong support for accreditation from his or her boss will have a very difficult time. Some standards transcend the police department and require cooperation from other government offices: personnel, budget, finance, and general services, for example. If this cooperation cannot be guaranteed, the accreditation process is likely to be extremely frustrating. Conversely, if interagency cooperation can be guaranteed, the accreditation process will not only further police goals but will also develop mutually beneficial relationships among all branches of government.

In addition, the community must be kept fully informed. Key leaders and associations should be brought on board early and should be kept apprised of progress. Broad-based community support provides a solid foundation for the challenging accreditation process.

The chief cannot relax. Within the agency, he or she must keep accreditation in the forefront and must also keep the police labor group informed of the progress of the effort and of its significance. Labor support will ensure that the agency's rank-and-file do not feel isolated or left out.

The accreditation manager   A hidden cost of accreditation is personnel time. For smaller agencies, one part-time person can manage the process. In larger agencies, the accreditation manager needs a staff, including clerical and secretarial support. This commitment may seem large, but the rewards are well worth it.

Regardless of agency size, the accreditation manager is crucial to the process. He or she should be an energetic individual with a record of achievement in planning, organizing, and running programs. In addition to serving as a driving force, the accreditation manager must keep everyone inside and outside the agency up-to-date. If the most appropriate candidate for this position does not already hold high rank, the demonstration of the agency's commitment demands that the position be highly placed, with easy access to the top administrator.

An overview of the accreditation process

Once having made the decision to go forward, the chief will find the accreditation process composed of a set of logical steps:

1. After initial information has been obtained from CALEA, the first step is to file an application accompanied by a nominal fee.
2. Upon receipt of the application, CALEA determines whether the agency is eligible. If so, CALEA provides an Agency Profile Questionnaire (APQ) that elicits basic information. Included with this package is the commission's standards manual.
3. Upon receipt of the completed APQ, CALEA reconfirms eligibility and sends a self-assessment package. The package is tailored to the agency's size, responsibilities, and other factors specific to the applicant.
4. The applicant initiates the self-assessment. Through this process, the chief will learn what is necessary to bring the department into compliance, as well as the costs of doing so. If difficulties are apparent, the agency may request a time extension for self-assessment or may withdraw its application entirely.
5. If a monumental barrier to a particular standard is encountered, the chief may request a waiver; the request must be accompanied by a plan of action to eventually comply with the standard. Waivers are granted infrequently, as wholesale waivers undercut the intent and spirit of accreditation.
6. The self-assessment is submitted when (a) all waivers have been either resolved or filed pending a decision, (b) all plans of action have been complete, and (c) compliance with all other applicable standards have been documented.

7. After reviewing the documentation, CALEA staff sends an on-site assessment plan together with a timetable of events and suggested dates for accomplishing each one.
8. At this point, the agency sends the balance of the accreditation fee and comments on the on-site assessment plan.
9. CALEA nominates an assessment team consisting of a team leader and, depending on agency size, one or more additional members. The agency is entitled to review the names and biographies of proposed assessors and may apply for rejections based on cause.
10. The assessment team conducts an on-site inspection. In addition to reviewing documentation, the team holds a public hearing, conducts interviews inside and outside the department, and inspects and rides with working officers.
11. The assessment team conducts a summation conference with the agency's chief. This amounts to a preliminary assessment.
12. The assessment staff prepares a report for CALEA staff, with an executive summary to members of the commission.
13. Following final review and testimony by the agency's representative(s), CALEA decides whether to award accredited status.

Reaccreditation

When hard work, anxiety, and diligence result in accreditation, the community, as well as the department, takes rightful pride in the accomplishment. After this euphoria over the original award, however, there is an emotional letdown. In addition, as time passes, the well-oiled accreditation management and compliance team is dissipated by transfers, retirements, promotions, and new hires. Other priorities arise, new crises loom, and the department is tempted to become complacent. It is critically important to avoid this temptation, because *re*accreditation is only five years away. Failure to fight off complacency about having achieved accreditation can quickly lead to noncompliance with accreditation standards.

The beauty—and the challenge—of accreditation is that, like learning and professional growth, it is a never-ending process. Compliance means not only *getting* the department current and fine tuned, but *keeping* it that way. The annual budget process, organizational changes, and new plans come to be examined in relation to the standards. Compliance puts rationality and solid direction into the agency's activities.

The responsibility for monitoring and evaluating departmental activities in relation to accreditation should be set during the original planning. The position or unit responsible for these tasks, as well as its authority and duties, should be clearly established through written directives. At a minimum, the directives should require this unit or position to do the following:

1. Periodically inspect files, records, and activities required by CALEA standards to ensure continuous compliance.
2. Work to increase the percentage of optional standards with which the agency complies.
3. Maintain all files and records required by CALEA.
4. Act as agency liaison with CALEA and other accredited agencies.
5. Review all directives, orders, written procedures, and the like before they are issued, to ensure that compliance levels are not compromised.
6. Issue bulletins to keep all agency personnel abreast of accreditation developments and the benefits of accredited status.
7. Budget for reaccreditation payments; review and coordinate all budget requests related to maintaining or improving compliance with accreditation standards.
8. Complete and forward to CALEA all annual reports and other required documents.
9. Plan for on-site reaccreditation assessment, including public meetings, assessor reception, a tour of the agency, and any other requested or required activities.
10. Identify "high-risk" activities that require constant monitoring if compliance is to continue.
11. Establish the frequency with which each standard will be checked for continued compliance.
12. Identify standards that require periodic reports, review, or other action, and create a system to ensure that reminders are sent and reports received.
13. Identify logistical support necessary for continual monitoring, and request the requisite staff, office space, furniture, and equipment.

The monitoring function should literally begin on the day after CALEA's assessment team finishes its work. The monitoring unit should pay particular attention to the suggestions made by the assessors or by the commission concerning areas in which compliance was perceived to be weak.

Within the first three months after accreditation, the monitoring unit should submit to management a master plan for continuing accreditation. This document will become the blueprint for the next five years and should include key dates with emphasis on budgeting for reaccreditation, payment of CALEA fees and expenses, annual reports, and periodic reports to management. This document is, in effect, a contract that will provide continuity as personnel changes occur.

Despite the establishment of a monitoring function with specific responsibilities, of course, the department's hierarchy cannot wash its hands of this process. Compliance is everybody's job, but top management bears the lion's share of responsibility for seeing to it that compliance is achieved and that it continues.

Benefits of accreditation

It should be clear by now that accreditation is not easy. So why should any law enforcement agency voluntarily go through this exercise? The answer is simple: departments find that the benefits of accreditation far outweigh the effort and costs it involves.

A CALEA survey found that 3,000 randomly selected law enforcement leaders placed improved organization and administration through self-assessment at the top of the list of benefits derived from going through the accreditation process. A close second was enhanced and updated rules, regulations, and policies.

According to the survey, other accreditation benefits that accrued to the agency included increased recognition and professional approval, enhanced accountability and professional performance, improved public relations, savings in the costs of liability insurance and litigation, improved employee morale and pride in the agency, and greater official response to budgetary and fiscal requests.

In most instances, the benefits of accreditation for individuals in the agency closely paralleled those cited in the survey for the agency as a whole. For example, the number one individual benefit cited was that accreditation provided employees with an excellent roadmap for good operations and a well-organized agency. Personal satisfaction, career development, professionalism, prestige, public relations, high morale, reduced stress, and budget justification also were identified.

Comments from leaders of accredited agencies and their state and local government officials support these findings and in some instances add new dimensions to the positive impact of accreditation. Consider Covington, Georgia, for example. In going through the accreditation process, the police department developed an internal personnel system. The city, recognizing the need for a personnel office, then created a personnel program of its own. When the department in Henrico County, Virginia, undertook the accreditation process, other county departments began asking the county manager if they could do self-evaluations or form citizens' panels or "something like the commission" to objectively evaluate themselves. In Schaumburg, Illinois, police department accreditation activities led to a collective bargaining agreement, and the rank-and-file's commitment to excellence created the impetus for a merit pay agreement.

New chiefs see accreditation as a way to measure their departments and to correct deficiencies when necessary. Where scandal or discord has tarnished an agency's image, accreditation is a way to rebuild trust and credibility. The chief of the first agency to be accredited—the Mount Dora, Florida, police department—attests that accreditation made the difference in his department, where the former chief had been convicted of theft and forgery and distrust of the police was rampant. Officers' morale bounced back, citizens showed their confidence by reporting more crimes, and even the change in departmental leadership came about smoothly.

In Buffalo Grove, Illinois, the police chief reports that the accreditation process caused his personnel to recognize previously unrealized strengths. "We learned a lot about the staff, and it was a good staff development exercise," he told the commission.

The Baltimore County experience

The Baltimore County Police Department became involved in the accreditation process early on. Employing 1,513 sworn personnel, 216 civilians, and 19 cadets, the department ranks 26th in size nationwide. The department participated in the field testing of early accreditation standards and became one of the first departments to become accredited.

The Baltimore County Police Department has enjoyed a wide variety of benefits during its first four years of accredited status:

1. Accreditation has provided a yardstick for measuring efficiency and effectiveness and has been an invaluable tool in the effort to stay continuously committed to the pursuit of excellence.
2. The accreditation standards helped the department refine previously existing directives and procedures. They also help prevent the issuance of directives that are inconsistent with commission standards.
3. Certain standards paralleled the direction in which the department was already moving. Complying with several other standards (career development, performance appraisal system, crime analysis, management reporting) has assisted staff in redesigning existing programs or creating new ones.
4. The standards have focused attention on specific inadequacies, most notably the department's holding cells, and have helped convince elected officials to respond to requests for funds to correct them.
5. Public respect and support for police have increased, as citizens have come to realize that they are being served by an agency that meets a demanding national level of excellence.
6. Local government officials point to the agency's accredited status in their economic development efforts. Entrepreneurs,

investors, managers, employees, and customers all are concerned with the quality of life and the level of public safety where they do business. A law enforcement agency that has demonstrated its excellence is one of a local government's most valuable assets.

7. Networking with others interested in accreditation has improved relations with other law enforcement and criminal justice agencies. Early on, the department was continually asked to assist other agencies as they went through the accreditation process. Later, this became a two-way street, and exchanges of information on exemplary programs and better ways of operating have worked to the mutual benefit of the departments involved.

8. Accreditation is a useful tool in the highly competitive area of recruitment. Exemplary, educated candidates look for an agency that is professional and that continues to strive for excellence. Accreditation makes it easier to bring highly qualified young people into the ranks.

9. Accreditation standards help justify budget requests for improved salaries and equipment. Community leaders and government officials are favorably influenced by justifications based on accreditation compliance.

10. Some benefits have proven intangible. Employees have more pride and motivation working for an accredited agency. Managers strive for a higher level of excellence, and the department's credo is being the best, rather than doing just enough to get by.

11. Compliance has helped reduce vicarious liability suits. When such suits do occur, the department is far better prepared to present evidence that virtually everything its officers do is based on standards that define nationally recognized and accepted practice. It is difficult for plaintiffs' lawyers to argue that departmental standards are deficient when they conform to the state of the art of American policing.

12. Compliance with particular standards helps in handling unusual occurrences. Emergency plans fine tuned by accreditation proved of great benefit when the department was faced with a train wreck that killed 16 people and injured 198 others.

13. Application of standards to vehicle pursuit and deadly force policies and procedures has kept the department abreast of modern concepts.

14. A recently issued CALEA standard covering the training of field training officers pointed out a previously unrecognized weakness and has helped the department make tangible improvements in recruit training.

The evolution continues

In its brief existence, accreditation for law enforcement has proven to be an achievable goal for both large and small police agencies. Accredited agencies include sheriff's departments, transit police, campus police, and state police. The program crossed national boundaries when the police department in the Canadian city of Edmonton, Alberta, was accredited. Thus, accreditation applies wherever there is a commitment to police excellence.

At this writing, more than one hundred agencies have been accredited, and more than seven hundred others are working their way through the accreditation process. We are at a milestone in policing. Professional status is an achievement that must be recognized and granted by independent and unbiased peers. Our colleagues who labor in the accreditation process are such a group, and their work can only change policing in ways that benefit the society of which we are a part.

1. Wickersham Commission (National Commission on Law Observance), *Wickersham Commission Reports, no. 14: Report on Police* (Washington, DC: U.S. Government Printing Office, 1931; Montclair, NJ: Patterson Smith, 1968).

2. August K. Vollmer, *Police and Modern Society* (Berkeley: University of California Press, 1936; Montclair, NJ: Patterson Smith, 1971).

3. Orlando W. Wilson, *Police Administration* (New York: McGraw-Hill, 1950).

4. President's Commission on Law Enforcement and Administration of Justice, *Task Force Report: The Po-* *lice* (Washington, DC: U.S. Government Printing Office, 1967).

5. National Advisory Commission on Criminal Justice Standards and Goals, *Police* (Washington, DC: U.S. Government Printing Office, 1973).

6. American Bar Association, *Standards Relating to the Urban Police Function* (New York: Institute of Judicial Administration, 1973).

7. *Manual of Correctional Standards*, 3d ed. (Washington, DC: American Correctional Association, 1966).

8. *Standards for Law Enforcement Agencies* (Fairfax, VA: Commission on Accreditation for Law Enforcement Agencies, Inc., 1983).

PART 4

Police Personnel and Training Issues

Professionalism through Police Supervisory Training

Vincent Henry and Sean Grennan

For good reason, the most important step in a police career is generally thought to be the move from the line to a first-line supervisory position. Newly promoted police supervisors often find it difficult to exercise authority over other officers, to give orders, to assume responsibility for the behavior of other officers, and, perhaps most painful, to discipline those who have so recently been their colleagues and peers.

Having cleared this initial hurdle, those who move from first-line supervisory positions to middle-management slots as lieutenants must make new adjustments.[1] Typically, they must supervise supervisors, serve as interpreters and conduits of information and directives that flow up and down the chain of command and between their departments and the public, and plan and coordinate large scale police operations.

While lengthy experience as a police officer certainly makes it easier for one to understand the how and why of supervisory and middle-management responsibilities, this experience alone is inadequate preparation for such jobs. Experience should be supplemented by formal supervisory and management training.

Various authorities have commented on the need for such systematic learning and developmental experiences. Detailed descriptions or analyses of such courses of study, however, are conspicuously absent from the literature of policing. As a consequence, instead of building on an existing base of knowledge, police officials intent on providing effective and job-relevant supervisory and man-

An earlier version of this paper was presented at the 1987 annual meeting of the American Society of Criminology in Montreal, Canada.

agement training courses frequently must begin building their courses from scratch.

This article attempts to fill some of the information void concerning supervisory and management training. It describes and analyzes the content of courses offered newly promoted sergeants and lieutenants in the nation's three largest police departments, and offers recommendations that may be useful to police administrators and researchers elsewhere in departments of all sizes.

The state of police training

American police training, in general, has made significant strides in recent years, and each stride has been a step toward further professionalization and away from the stereotype of the "dumb cop." As Charles B. Saunders, Jr., notes, there is a general failure within society to recognize that policing is a complex and demanding occupation, requiring of its practitioners a high order of skills and intelligence. This misconception contributes to the problems of the police, and partially explains the lack of public support for efforts to upgrade standards of police personnel, education, and training.[2] Saunders cites Raymond Fosdick, whose *American Police Systems* is generally credited as the first scholarly assessment of the American police:

[T]he quality of a department's work depends on the observation, knowledge, discretion, courage, and judgment of the men, acting as individuals ... Only as the training of the policeman is deliberate and thorough, with emphasis on the social implications and human aspects of his task, can real success in police work be achieved.[3]

Certainly, some things have changed since Fosdick wrote, but the "social implications and human aspects" of policing, or of police supervision and management, surely have not diminished. As Weston notes, police supervision is a "social relationship" in which subordinates' behavior is shaped and controlled through the interpersonal processes of persuasion, suggestion, and direction.[4] Because the police officers who are subjects of such control efforts are themselves expert at manipulating others through such processes, this is no easy task. To deal effectively with the ambiguous situations that characterize much of their work, police officers rely upon intuition, negotiation, and coercion.[5] In time, they become highly sensitized to others' attempts to influence them through the same mechanisms. When they view such attempts or their purposes as unreasonable, they may, subtly or overtly, subvert them. Consequently, police supervisors' jobs—manipulating those who are more accustomed to manipulating others—demand that they be flexible enough to pick and choose the least obtrusive supervisory technique likely to be successful. Unfortunately, one of the most commonly recognized problems within police organizations is a level of management flexibility inadequate to choose and alternate among these operating techniques.[6] As a consequence, many police managers coerce when negotiation is more appropriate. Perhaps less often, others refrain from coercion even when it is clearly necessary. In their inflexibility, such managers limit their own effectiveness and, equally important, may encourage subordinates to inflexibility in their dealings with citizens.

The effective supervisor is an expert communicator, a leader, and a motivator who understands the psychological aspects of supervisors' social relationship with subordinates.[7] Each of these supervisory attributes is directly tied to a social relationship or social skill. It follows, therefore, that a well-conceived, job relevant supervisory training program must concentrate on expanding and refining these skills. In our constantly evolving and increasingly complex society, the need for socially attuned and responsive police officers, supervisors and managers cannot be ignored. Indeed, it is greater today than when Fosdick published his work in 1920.

The realities of modern policing require that the police possess certain attributes or, at least, the capacity to develop them. James Q. Wilson notes that considerable time and effort have been devoted to devising methods of identifying men and women who are suited to police work by virtue of possessing this capacity, but that police training programs are generally ineffective in developing it. Instead, he asserts, police training programs often "emphasize memorization of legal codes and department rules more than the development of skills for managing conflict."[8] But, according to Bittner, the great majority of street situations encountered by police are resolved without strict reliance upon rules, regulations, or laws.[9]

Further, Wilson argues, even the process of training officers in law and formalized procedure is accomplished inefficiently. Individualized, programmed instruction, he claims, would be more effective than that traditional lecture method upon which most police training relies. The object of this training, he states, should be to develop in the trainee:

an inner sense of competence and self assurance so that . . . the officer is capable of responding flexibly and in a dispassionate manner rather than rigidly, emotionally or defensively. These objectives will not be accomplished by simply multiplying courses that, seriatum, take upon the law, department rules, . . . and human development.[10]

To the extent that these criticisms of police training are valid, they point out especially grievous weaknesses in the training of police supervisors and managers, who must serve as role models, trainers, and mentors to rank-and-file officers. Further, since effective and professional police response results from a combination of theoretical and practical considerations, there is also a place for formal education (as opposed to vocational training) in development of police supervisors and managers. Police supervisors and managers, Stolovich and McDonald point out, must rapidly analyze and dissect situations prior to implementing department policy. This set of skills, they continue, is best acquired through a combination of a broad educational background, formal and job-specific classroom training, and practical on-the-job training.[11]

The classroom training setting allows for discussion and simulation of theoretical situations in a relatively low-risk environment, while situation-based training allows for adaptation and application of such theories to actual incidents. The uncontested value of a broad educational background aside,[12] the classroom approach to management development and training also allows for acquisition of theoretical knowledge, while procedural, on-the-job training provides the necessary nuts-and-bolts information.

Despite the evident logic and social benefits of hiring, retaining, and promoting intelligent officers and training them well, police training has been hampered by inability to precisely define the factors that combine to create effective, dynamic, and successful officers. Most certainly, the factors or criteria that define competent and able police supervisors and managers have yet to be identified more satisfactorily than our own general prescriptions for flexibility and social awareness. In the absence of standards more specific than these, much police training is haphazard, and based on educated guesses at the qualities of the good supervisor or manager, rather than on empirically verifiable realities.

Supervisory and management training

Merely by virtue of their experience in training great numbers of supervisors and middle managers, one might expect the municipal police departments of Chicago, Los Angeles, and New York to have made the most accurate assessments of the appropriate content of supervisory and management training. Our own observations of the work of these three departments also suggest that, aside from minimal and idiosyncratic differences in policies and procedures, the similarities among the departments, and of the work of the supervisors and managers in them, greatly outweigh the differences among them. Consequently, and even though these cities and their police departments have very different histories and traditions, one might also expect to find great similarities in supervisory and management training among them.

To examine the supervisory and management training programs of these three departments, data related to their most recent courses of instruction for new sergeants and lieutenants were requested and obtained.

Syllabi and attendance data for a total of six courses (sergeant and lieutenant in each department) were collated and analyzed. Many factors affect training quality, but some (e.g., degree of instructors' preparedness, command of language, ability to communicate; nature of physical surroundings) are virtually impossible to quantify. Consequently, this article focuses on three variables: number of instructional hours; topics of instruction; and number of students.

Table 1 illustrates that, in terms of these three variables, training for new sergeants is extremely similar across these three cities. All three departments offer courses of 140 hours' duration that cover a large number of topics (58 in Chicago; 54 each in Los Angeles and New York). As one might expect, the size of sergeants' classes, like that of lieutenants' classes, increases with department size. At the lieutenant rank, the training effort appears to be greatest in Los Angeles. Newly promoted LAPD lieutenants participate in a 120 hour course, versus 49 and 35 hours, respectively, for Chicago and New York.[13]

Sergeants' training
Chicago   The "Pre-Service Training Course" offered by the Chicago Police Department (CPD) is a four-week, 140-hour course administered in two phases.

Phase I consists of 70 instructional hours administered over two weeks, and emphasizes technical and procedural skills. This first stage of training is presented primarily in a lecture format, and is characterized by a nuts-and-bolts approach to supervision (and to training) that emphasizes such topics as "The Performance Rating System," "Medical Policy and Procedure," and "The Field Responsibilities of Patrol Sergeants." A notable exception to the

Table 1. Characteristics of police supervisory and middle management training programs.

City	Hours of instruction	Trainees per class	Topics of instruction
Chicago			
Sergeants	140	25	58
Lieutenants	49	15-20	21
Los Angeles			
Sergeants	140	20	54
Lieutenants	120	6-8	27
New York			
Sergeants	140	75-100	54
Lieutenants	35	30-70	23

mechanistic tone of this phase is the inclusion of a four hour "Sergeant's Transition Panel," in which trainees meet with a panel of experienced sergeants in order to learn at first hand what to expect in their new roles. This panel includes a question-and-answer session and is scheduled for the last day of the training phase.

During these two weeks, the new sergeants also view three hours of videotaped simulated police shooting incidents and critique the incidents in terms of legality, department policy, and appropriateness of officers' actions. Two hours of lecture on complaints made against members of the department are followed by a five-hour practicum in which each new sergeant conducts a mock investigation and hearing, including the preparation of necessary paperwork. New sergeants also receive instruction in the duties and responsibilities of their own supervisors, the field lieutenants. This strategy is aimed at fostering cooperation and understanding across the supervisory ranks.

After two months of field experience, new CPD sergeants return to the training academy to participate in Phase II, "Personnel Concerns." The topics included in this 70-hour phase are oriented toward interpersonal dynamics, motivation, leadership, and personnel development. Emphasis is on enhancing the supervisor's communication skills and the utilization of personnel and other departmental resources. During this phase, extensive use is made of guest speakers from outside the department, and classes vary from lectures through discussions to group participation exercises.

Representative of the topics included in this phase is a 14-hour instructional block entitled "Interpersonal Skills for Effective Employee Diagnosis and Coaching Interviews: Non-Verbal Behavior and the Coaching Process." This block stresses the development of interview skills and the interpretation of subtle non-verbal cues in evaluating subordinates' performance. Other topics included in Phase II include "Police Motivational Characteristics" and "Leadership and Motivational Concepts."

The problems of alcoholic and emotionally disturbed officers are also addressed in Phase II, as are the professional counseling services available through the department to such officers. Actual case studies and realistic videotaped scenarios are employed throughout this training.

CPD reports that class size in both phases of the Pre-Service Sergeants' Course averages 25, regardless of the number of sergeants appointed at any particular time.

Los Angeles LAPD's 140-hour Supervisory Development Course is an uninterrupted four-week program that must be completed before promotion to sergeant. Appropriately, this program begins with a

"Transition Panel" that focuses on the differences between the police officer's responsibility to do the work and the supervisor's responsibility of getting police officers to do the work.

The Supervisory Development Course includes no more than 20 participants, and uses intensive training sessions that concentrate on one topic per day. These blocks are divided into shorter sub-topics, but a continuity of subject matter is maintained throughout the day. A full day session of "Counseling" training, for example, consists of eight subtopics, including "Crisis Intervention," "Stress and Its Impact on Law Enforcement," and "Process and Procedures in Counseling." Other full day training blocks include "Communication," "Press Relations," and a total of three days devoted to "Leadership." A day of training in public speaking and another in the supervisory training function are also provided.

Benefits of the full day training blocks are the flexibility and informality they allow. Discussions are not limited and instructors are not confined by the rigid schedules characteristic of police training programs that closely adhere to military style, hour-by-hour lesson plan formats. Instead, at instructors' discretion, particularly productive discussions or workshops can be permitted to exceed usual time guidelines, and skilled instructors may segue into new topics without interrupting the rate or flow of learning.

LAPD has also incorporated standardized self-assessment instruments and questionnaires into its supervisory training. After completion and scoring, these analytic tools enable new supervisors to gain insights into their own supervisory strengths, to diagnose weaknesses, and to choose leadership styles and techniques that complement their own personalities.

The final week of training includes three full day modules in "Leadership," "Tactics," and "Integrating Leadership and Tactics." Sergeant trainees are expected to master these subjects, drawing on course materials and putting their theoretical training to practical use. The final day of the training is a critique both of the course and of individual trainees. Trainees discuss their self-assessment profiles and prepare written career plans with the assistance of expert instructors. A written examination tests trainees' knowledge of course material, and a formal inspection concludes the course.

The syllabus for the Supervisory Development Course indicates that a majority of the topics (60 percent) are presented in interactive training sessions rather than through traditional lectures. Trainee participation is geared toward practice in realistic simulated situations. In the "Disciplinary Investigation Procedures" training block, for example, each trainee actually conducts a mock personnel complaint investigation, interviewing witnesses and complainants, and completing all necessary paperwork.

New York   NYPD's Basic Management Orientation Course (BMOC) is provided to newly appointed sergeants over a five week period and interposes formal classroom training with supervised field experience. The first week of training, conducted at the Police Academy, consists of 35 instructional hours designed to familiarize new promotees with the basic duties and responsibilities of station house officers and patrol supervisors. Guest speakers from various departmental units (e.g., the Property Clerk Division and the Legal Division) present many of the lectures. During this week, the new sergeants hear two-hour lectures on such topics as "Desk Duties," "Posting the Platoon," and "Log Entries." Perhaps surprisingly, only one hour during this week is devoted to "Leadership Styles" and, in contrast to LAPD's great emphasis on leadership in its new sergeants' course, the entire BMOC devotes only two hours to this topic.

After this first week, new sergeants are sent to the field for an additional week of training at the hands of experienced sergeants in the boroughs and precincts to which they will be assigned.[14] Following this practical experience, new sergeants return to the training academy for another 35 hours of training designed to teach application of management concepts to job situations. This third BMOC training phase includes three five-hour interactive blocks on "Training," "Public Speaking," and viewing and critiquing a training film ("It's Your Move, Sergeant") that presents a variety of supervisory problems. The remaining 20 hours of this phase consist of lectures.

The fourth and final phase of BMOC attempts to develop new supervisors' personal leadership styles and to apply course material to field situations. Among the topics covered in this 35-hour segment are seven hours of "Supervisory Workshops," the remaining hour of "Leadership," two hours on "Decision Making," and a three-hour orientation to the department's computer system and its value to supervisors.

In all, NYPD's approach to sergeant training differs considerably from the programs in Chicago and Los Angeles. Both CPD and LAPD provide new sergeants with 140 classroom contact hours, but NYPD's 140 hour program includes only 105 classroom hours. Further, except for the 35 hour field training segment including in the BMOC program, there is comparatively little direct interaction between instructors and trainees in NYPD's training for new sergeants: more than 85 of the 105 classroom hours are delivered in a traditional lecture format rather than in the more personalized modes recommended by Wilson[15] and others. In addition, the impersonality of the BMOC course frequently is exacerbated by mass promotions that, in recent courses, have dictated class sizes that exceed more than 100 trainees per instructor and have increased reliance on the lecture format.

Lieutenants' training

Chicago   CPD provides a seven-day, 49-hour course of instruction for new lieutenants. The program, about half of which is conducted by trainers from outside CPD, includes lectures, workshops, and discussions. It is usually offered to classes of 15 or 20.

Among the course's major topics are a seven-hour block of instruction called "Leadership Concepts," which emphasizes situational leadership roles. Promotees also confer with veteran lieutenants in a four-hour "Transition Panel," but the primary emphasis of the course is on specific procedures, duties, and tasks. About a quarter of the course deals with lieutenants' personnel responsibilities, and much of the rest includes such topics as "Payroll and Timekeeping Issues," "Watch Commander/Field Lieutenant Duties," and "Department Fleet Safety."

Los Angeles   LAPD uses a bifurcated program of instruction in training new lieutenants in groups of six or eight. One phase of this system is the "Peace Officer Standards and Training (POST) Management Course" mandated by the state of California. The second phase, conducted in-house, is simply called "Lieutenant's School."

The POST course is usually given prior to the LAPD program and includes 75 hours of instruction over ten days. The course is conducted by academic personnel at California State University at Northridge and employs an impressive required reading list that focuses on practical applications of management theories and philosophies, rather than on procedural issues. Each day in the POST program is devoted to a broad topic that, as in the LAPD sergeant's program, is then divided into smaller subtopics. These full day sessions involve such concepts as "Social Change and Managerial Responsibility," "The Evolving Legal Environment," and "The Complexities of Leadership." One full day is also devoted to management analysis and to critiques of filmed case studies. Self-assessment instruments and interactive discussion groups are employed throughout the POST training.

Phase II of this program, LAPD's Lieutenant's School, is a five-day, 40-hour program that covers 26 topics. This part of the program also addresses general management issues (e.g., "Employee Relations," "Values and Principles," "Effective Communication"). In large measure, however, this is a procedurally oriented course of study designed to take up where the POST offering has left off; most of it consists of subjects such as "Divisional Jail Management," "Management of Roll Call Training," "Sick and Injured On-Duty Management," and "Unusual Occurrence Procedures."

New York   NYPD's "Lieutenant Orientation Course" (LOC) devotes approximately 35 hours to training newly appointed lieutenants. The course is presented as a series of lectures, most of which are delivered by speakers from various units within the department. These include the police commissioner and several of his top aides.

In many ways, the course reflects NYPD's ambiguity over the organizational role of the lieutenant. Class size (30 to 70) is far larger than is true of Chicago or Los Angeles, and a recent class of newly promoted lieutenants participated in the same class sessions as did a group of newly promoted captains. Table 2 shows that course content is also subject to considerable variation.

Table 2. Topics and instructional hours in two consecutive NYPD lieutenant orientation courses.

	Hours of instruction		
Topic	August[1]	September[1]	Change
Legal Division	3	3	0
Internal Affairs Division	1	1	0
Office of Labor Policy	2	2	0
Desk Duties[2]	2	2	0
Chief of Patrol (speech)	1	n/o[3]	−
Media and Press Relations	1.5	n/o	−
Police Commissioner (speech)	0.5	n/o	−
Bias Incident Investigation	1.5	n/o	−
Managing Civilian Employees	1.5	1	−
Writing Workshop[2]	2	1.5	−
Administrative Duties[2]	1.5	1	−
Inspections Division	1.5	1	−
Computer System	5	1	−
Civilian Complaint Review Bd.	1	2	+
Chief of Department (speech)	1	2	+
Property Clerk Division	2	3	+
Drug Awareness[2]	2	2.5	+
Department Advocate's Office	1	1.5	+
Felony Augmentation Program	1	1.5	+
Lieutenant's Benevolent Assoc.	n/o	0.5	+
College Liaison Unit	n/o	1	+
Equal Employment Opportunity	n/o	1.5	+
Delegating Authority	n/o	1	+
Employee Relations Unit	n/o	1	+
TOTAL	33	33.5	

[1]August 1986 class included lieutenants and captains; September 1986 class was lieutenants only.
[2]Instruction by Police Academy staff; all other instruction by speakers from specialized department unit involved.
[3]n/o = not offered.

More specifically, the August LOC covered 19 topics in 33 hours. The following month's LOC (offered to a combined class of lieutenants and captains), however, deleted four of these topic areas (speeches by the police commissioner and the chief of patrol, "Media and Press Relations," "Bias Incident Investigation"); added five new ones ("Lieutenants' Benevolent Association," "College Liaison Unit," "Equal Employment Opportunity," "Delegating Authority," and "Employee Relations Unit"); subtracted from the time devoted to nine others, and added to the time spent on the remaining 11. In all, the time devoted to only four topic areas remained unchanged between these two consecutive programs.

Conclusions

The intent of the authors in conducting this research has not been to point out specific inadequacies in the training programs examined. Instead, we have attempted to provide information that may be useful in construction or review of training programs for new police sergeants and lieutenants. These are three large departments that have served bellwether roles in training and personnel development and that may have research and personnel resources not available to smaller departments. The roles of supervisors and middle managers in very large urban departments may differ somewhat from those played by their colleagues in smaller jurisdictions, but the fundamental organizational and managerial issues they face vary only slightly. Further, there is very little reason to believe that training objectives or methods should vary much with department size. Hence, there may be valuable lessons in the experiences of these three big departments.

Interagency variation   One lesson is that even these three departments differ substantially on the major emphases of their courses. NYPD's BMOC program devotes a total of two hours to "Leadership," a seemingly critical issue that is the subject of three full days of instruction in the comparable LAPD course. Half (70 hours) of Chicago's training for new sergeants falls under the generic heading of "Personnel Concerns," a subject which is covered in four hours in NYPD, and in three days in LAPD.

Supervisory training as part of the developmental experience   These courses are, of course, only part of the socialization and experiences that prepare new sergeants for their jobs, and there is no way to determine in a study of limited scope how—or how well—each department's training course complements those other experiences. If one assumes that the content of these three new sergeants' courses has each been determined by a thorough needs analysis, however, one must conclude that each course meets its department's particular needs. One should also expect, therefore, that well-thought-out supervisory and middle-management courses that fill the specific needs of smaller police departments will also have their own unique characteristics. Consequently, in designing supervisory and management training, other agencies are probably well-advised to give primary attention to their own needs and to use other departments' syllabi as little more than general guidelines that may or may not be relevant.

Agency-specific training   In addition, one would also expect that supervisory training courses offered to many police departments by, for example, state or regional training authorities will not fully meet the needs of any single participating police agency. In such cases, as with LAPD's Supervisory Development Course (taught in part by California State University at Northridge under state POST requirements), the departments involved should supplement such lowest common denominator training with their own in-house programs. Again, mechanisms of socialization and experience unique to each agency probably make multi-agency training courses more valuable to some departments than to others.

Defining the job   Another lesson is suggested by NYPD's experiences in training lieutenants. This training (35 hours according to course syllabi; somewhat less in the two actual sessions described) is far less than that provided by CPD (49 hours) or LAPD (120 hours). In addition, it fluctuated greatly in the two consecutive sessions we examined and, in one case, was apparently indistinguishable from a pre-promotion to captain course that was in progress at the same time.

This flux, we conclude, is probably attributable to the absence of a clear definition of the NYPD lieutenant's job. Consequently, it suggests strongly that, before attempting to develop training courses for personnel at any organizational level, police agencies should remove as much ambiguity as possible from position descriptions.

Teaching methods and logistics   Questions of class size and training method are inextricably woven together. The literature of policing, and the literature of adult pedagogy generally, have by now made it clear that interactive training methods are preferable to lectures. In such sessions, trainees are comfortable, can pose questions, engage in dialogue, and synthesize subject matter into their own experiences and cognitive bases. Questions and observations that might be stifled in large group settings are more likely to be verbalized in small groups and are easily addressed by instructors in such settings. Thus, the large classes characteristic of NYPD's supervisory and middle-management courses probably limit instructors' capacity to deliver effective training, as well as trainees' ability to internalize it.

This problem, the authors know from observations elsewhere, is not unique to New York City. Nor, in most cases, is such large class size—in either recruit or pre-promotion training courses—typically the result of police departments' preference. Instead, it is usually caused by irregularities in hiring and promotion which are attributable to economic, political, or legal matters beyond the control of police administrators. This pattern of training valleys and peaks—an empty training academy and idle staff suddenly overwhelmed with large numbers of trainees—however, has extremely deleterious effects on both trainers and trainees, and police officials should do whatever they can to avoid it.

Transition panels   The use of these panels by CPD and LAPD is an excellent idea. New sergeants, especially, often are subject to misconceptions and trepidation about their new roles. A transition panel composed of credible, experienced supervisors can be a useful device to orient and educate the trainees. Like the mentor programs from which they derive (and which also inspire NYPD's field training experience for new sergeants), they are a proven and effective training device. Informal conversations with police supervisors and middle managers disclose that the panels are a viable and valuable way of minimizing promotees' anxiety and its effect on their work.

Self-assessment   Another useful training strategy is seen in LAPD's use of self-assessment instruments. These self-administered paper-and-pencil tests are fairly reliable measures of individual personality traits and are widely used in management and executive training and development programs in and out of government. It seems appropriate that police training administrators consider their adoption in supervisory and middle-management training as well.

In this brief article, we have outlined the forms of supervisory and middle-management training followed by the nation's three largest police departments. Like their cities and their traditions, the programs differ somewhat, and none is perfect. Still, each program reflects a good faith effort to do what is best for the public, for trainees, and for the officers they will lead upon successful completion of training. Each is also a starting point for police administrators who seek to develop or refine their own supervisory and middle management training.

1. The position of police captain is also typically considered to be one of middle management. It will be excluded from this discussion, however, on grounds that it is more appropriately viewed as an entry-level executive position than as one with direct supervisory responsibilities over line workers.

2. Charles B. Saunders, Jr., *Upgrading the American Police* (Washington, DC: The Brookings Institution, 1970), pp. 13–14.

3. Raymond Fosdick, *American Police Systems* (New York: Century Co., 1920), p. 306.

4. Paul B. Weston, *Supervision in the Administration of Justice: Police, Corrections, Courts* (Springfield, IL: Charles C Thomas, 1965), p. 6.

5. See, for example, Egon Bittner, *The Functions of the Police in Modern Society* (Rockville, MD: National Institute of Mental Health, 1970); William Ker Muir, *Police: Streetcorner Politicians* (Chicago: University of Chicago Press, 1977); Albert J. Reiss, Jr., *The Police and the Public* (New Haven: Yale University Press, 1971).

6. Dorothy Guyot, "Bending Granite: Attempts to Change the Rank Structure of American Police Departments," *Journal of Police Science and Administration* 7 (1979): 253.

7. Weston, *Supervision in the Administration of Justice*, p. 7.

8. James Q. Wilson, *Thinking About Crime*, second edition (New York: Vintage Books, 1983), p. 111.

9. Bittner, *The Functions of the Police*, pp. 52–62.

10. Wilson, *Thinking About Crime*, p. 112.

11. Harold D. Stolovich and Victor N. McDonald, "A Quasi-Policy Statement on the Role of Formal Management Training and Education in Police Management Development," *Canadian Police College Journal* 5 (1981): 81-97.

12. We concur absolutely with Stolovich and McDonald (and many others) about the value of a broad academic background to police personnel at all levels. For a variety of reasons, however, we have elected to confine the substance of the remainder of this article to discussion of training delivered or sponsored by police agencies.

13. The comparatively low number of training hours provided for NYPD lieutenants is probably attributable, at least in part, to the poor definition of the lieutenant's position. In Chicago, lieutenants are eligible for discretionary appointments to high command ranks and have held such positions as commander of the training academy and, indeed, even as superintendent. LAPD lieutenants typically hold important command positions and routinely serve as watch commanders. In NYPD, however, the lieutenant's position is only vaguely distinguishable from that of sergeant. Indeed, over the junior author's career in NYPD, rumors that the rank of lieutenant was to be abolished seemed to arise every few years.

14. For police purposes, New York City's five boroughs are divided into seven borough commands (Manhattan South; Manhattan North; Bronx; Brooklyn South; Brooklyn North; Queens; and Staten Island). Seventy-five precincts, the fundamental NYPD command unit, are spread across the seven boroughs.

15. Wilson, *Thinking About Crime*, p. 112.

Alienation among Veteran Police Officers

— Mark Pogrebin

A common problem for most police department managers is the perceived low productivity rates for veteran officers at the line level. This study addresses the causes for older patrol officers' feelings of alienation and hostility toward the police organization, which tend to give supervisors the impression that these officers are marginal employees.

Problem employees

In a study that attempted to identify and characterize unproductive police officers, Robinette found that they are predominantly male, assigned to patrol or investigations, and have some college education.[1] They tend to be between 30 and 34 years old, with six to 10 years of police employment. Robinette notes that as police officers reach their thirties, they have already adjusted their job expectations, modifying motivation and job performance patterns and becoming more resistant to change. Police officers in this age category very often voice negative reactions toward any modifications that affect their routine (i.e., shift or job assignment changes), since change is often perceived as a threat to job stability. According to Robinette, veteran officers have a strong interest in maintaining stability by demanding that seniority be considered when organizational changes are proposed. They have a high degree of intolerance for new training programs and requirements for additional career-related formal education.

The attitudinal problems experienced by officers in this age bracket are compounded by the lack of promotional opportunities. Reiser found that, because the majority of police tend to be very competitive, failure to obtain anticipated promotions often resulted in feelings of organizational alienation, depression and loss of self-esteem.[2] Schwartz and Schwartz maintain that an officer who has six or more years of police employment and has not attained promotion often develops into a problem employee. They note that, despite how good an officer may have been, once he realizes that promotion will probably never occur, he may very likely become a destructive force within the department, perhaps opting to retire on the job and collect his pay until he reaches actual retirement.[3] A similar view is shared by Whisenand, who believes that older police officers become dissatisfied when their promotional expectations and salary increases do not materialize.[4]

According to Schwartz and Schwartz, there is an enormous waste of talent, resources and energy among line officers. Often, these members of the force "burn out" because of a perceived lack of managerial attention and a belief that they have been treated unfairly in the promotional process, with the result that they display a high degree of dissatisfaction for the job and the department. Such negative feelings on the part of veteran officers can often affect the entire organization, as officers with less tenure may become persuaded that good police work goes unrecognized and unrewarded.

In 1981, Clay and Yates conducted a study to analyze various types of police department employee problems, surveying police administrators nationally from five sessions of participants at the FBI National Academy.[5] Asked to identify the most significant problems among employees, 38.5 percent cited lackadaisical work effort ("doing just enough to get by"), 19.9 percent complained of absenteeism and tardiness, 11.2 percent mentioned resistance to change, and 30.4 percent cited other miscellaneous problems.

In attempting to assign responsibility for these problems, 39.9 percent of the administrators blamed the employee; 26.6 percent, outside influences; and 26.6 percent, organizational management. Only 6.6 percent of respondents considered the immediate supervisor to be the primary cause of employee problems. It is significant that only one out of four ranking administrators perceived himself as having any responsibility for marginal performance by his employees.

Performance evaluations

Most supervisory evaluations of a police officer's job performance are based on such criteria as number of arrests made, traffic citations issued, field interviews conducted, property inspections completed, crimes investigated and quality of written reports.[6] Very often, however, police complain that the criteria for performance evaluations are unclear. A further problem with the evaluation process is that non-tangible activities, such as citizen satisfaction with police performance in service activities, is not taken into account.[7] The absence of clearly formulated and agreed-upon criteria for measurement of performance tends to add to the uncertainty of line officers. As a result, productivity criteria become individualized among patrol officers.

Employees are often evaluated by a standard of performance of which they are unaware. This is a result of first-line supervisors not informing their subordinates of their productivity expectations at the beginning of the evaluation period. Although supervisors' expectations were once thought to have a negative effect on employee morale, Carey found this to be untrue: His study concluded that workers' morale levels actually increased when performance expectation levels were instituted.[8]

Subjective judgments of police performance on the part of first-line supervisors is one of the big complaints of veteran officers. It is no secret that police who are relatively new to the job usually have higher productivity levels than their more senior peers, since judgments made by veteran officers frequently result in nonenforcement approaches—giving a warning for a traffic violation, rather than a ticket, or defusing a tense situation through conflict resolution techniques rather than arrest. The less experienced officer who makes arrests and gives out traffic tickets thus ends up looking more productive than his veteran counterpart. Supervisors who rely heavily on such criteria to make comparisons among subordinates on their shift may unfairly judge more seasoned officers as being less productive.

Need for recognition

Veteran police often feel unappreciated by those in management positions. Preiss and Ehrlich have suggested that a desire for recognition has become a major goal of police officers.[9] There is a need for those working in line positions to believe that good work will be rewarded by recognition and compensation. Unfortunately, while routine good work is rarely recognized within police organizations, an officer *can* count on being reprimanded for poor performance.[10]

Personnel who remain in line positions, especially in patrol, are perceived by their managers as lacking ambition and motivation, even though they may have chosen specifically to stay in patrol. Veteran officers belong in this category. They have not been promoted to supervisory positions, whether by choice or not. Frequently, they find themselves working as subordinates for managers they themselves trained years ago. Seeing others move up in the police organization to management positions can affect the veteran line officer's perception of self worth, especially if he believes he was a better officer when they were of equal rank working on the same shift. Younger employees who ascend the organizational hierarchy rapidly tend to generate envy from their peers, who believe they have been passed over unfairly for promotion.[11] Sometimes this envy manifests itself in negative interpersonal contacts between the superior and his less-successful subordinates. This situation occurs daily if the first-line supervisor happens to manage the shift that a veteran officer works on. The result of such conflict between the younger supervisor and the older patrolman can last through the duration of the shift. However, there are ways in which management at all levels of the police department can diminish the resentment felt by the veteran officer.

Management and alienation

Police managers must perceive policing as a vocation that makes great demands on an officer's experience and judgment. Veteran officers have the experience needed to make appropriate judgments in the ambiguous situations that often occur, and managers must appreciate this fact. It is necessary for them to utilize the older officer's talents in making judgments that do not cause citizen dissatisfaction.

Because municipal law enforcement organizations are structured on a paramilitary model, it is difficult for administrators to allow individual officers' talents to become models for younger police. Continued reliance on authoritative methods of control tends to decrease the possibilities for police to experience psychological success and self-esteem.[12] Quite frequently, police managers attempt to treat their subordinates equally as a group; thus, little deference is paid to those police with years of experience. Such treatment can be attributed to the authoritative structure of police organizations, which views subordinates of similar rank as equals.

When older police are considered to be producing marginal work, managers must attempt to understand the reasons for their lack of productivity. Efforts must be made to resolve low performance, job dissatisfaction and overall negative attitude toward the department. In sum, police administrators must care enough about those in lower-ranking positions in order to make organizational changes that will remedy the problem. Administrative styles of management must reflect a philosophy of concern for employees. They must be sensitive to their subordinates' values and feelings. Unfortunately for the veteran police officer, this does not occur very often, nor do many policies exist that deal with career development after officers have been on the job for a number of years. The following study attempts to analyze the reasons for veteran officers' feelings of alienation from the police department, and supervisors' perceptions of veterans' low productivity rates.

Methods

This research project was conducted in a suburban police department with a total of 135 sworn officers, located in a Colorado city with a population of 96,000. The city is part of the metropolitan Denver area.

The study is based on six months' observation and multiple interviews with 20 veteran officers in the patrol bureau who were employed by the department for 10 years or more. Observations and numerous interviews were also conducted with the six shift supervisors to whom the 210 veteran officers were assigned. The average length of time employed for this sample was 12 years, and the officers' mean age was 35.

Analysis

The observation and interview process uncovered a number of complaints among these veteran officers concerning the job and the department. Included among these concerns were the following perceptions of unfair treatment on the part of management.

1. Shift selection and days off did not take seniority into account
2. Unfair promotional process
3. Supervisors showing little respect for older officers' experience
4. Methods of productivity measurement were unfair for veteran officers
5. Veteran officers were not requested to offer their expertise
6. Administrative insensitivity to the aging process of older officers.

Seniority and shift selection   Shift assignments in the department were made on a yearly basis. At the time this study was conducted, the administration implemented a policy stating that any patrol officer who served two consecutive years on any shift had to be moved to one of the other two shift assignments, the rationale being that all officers should have the opportunity to experience working different times and days during their employment. Also, manpower needs were becoming a problem in that the majority of veteran officers were working the day shift with weekends off. This left a real experience gap for the other two shifts, where the majority of criminal activity occurs.

The new policy angered the older officers, who felt that their seniority was all they had in the way of status. They realized the administration's purpose in rotating everyone to different shifts, but resented the demise of seniority's importance, which they had worked so hard to attain. For older police, the stability of working a permanent shift with the same days off tended to decrease family stress they would otherwise experience. They claimed that permanence on work assignment caused far fewer family problems.

Unfair promotional process   The majority of veterans had, at one time or another, attempted to participate in the sergeant's promotional process. Those who had tried for promotion most recently expressed the most hostility at not being selected. The written test was difficult for them and they were competing against college graduates who apparently had better writing skills. As a result of their low scores on the written exam, they never received the opportunity to compete in the last two promotional stages, which consisted of an oral exam and blind review conducted by supervisors.

A general feeling of despair seemed to descend on veteran officers when discussing their feelings about promotion. First, they had to reconcile themselves to the fact that they would never move up the rank structure; second, because they had not been promoted, they felt like failures in the eyes of the rest of the department, which led to low self-esteem. All they had left were special assignments, which were usually offered to officers who were well-thought-of by supervisors. This, for the most part, again left veteran officers out of contention.

Experience and respect   Next to the issue of shift assignment and days off, this area proved to be the biggest bone of contention for senior officers. Not one of the 20 veteran officers sampled perceived the organization as respecting the experience they had gained throughout their careers as police. They felt that past events in which their judgment and experience had proved invaluable meant little in their current situation. One reason for this was that many officers who were employed at the time these events occurred were either no longer with the department or had moved up to administrative positions, where they experience minimal contact with line officers. Thus, good police work in the past rarely is known to new supervisors and young patrol officers.

Based on observations, veteran officers appeared to handle dangerous incidents with less stress than their younger counterparts. In domestic interactions, veteran police very often utilized their skills for conflict resolution, diminishing the opportunities for violence to occur. Their verbal skills were called into play in these situations, and it was obvious that their years of experience were a tremendous asset. The same proved true in other situations encountered over the six-month study period. Yet despite the quality of their work, their negative attitudes seemed to cause strained relations with their superiors.

Report writing proved to be a particular problem among senior officers. It was not uncommon for shift supervisors to have to ask veterans to rewrite their reports and even remind them to use the proper form; in fact, failure to write incident reports properly was the biggest complaint sergeants expressed toward seasoned patrol officers.

Interestingly, it was learned that veteran police frequently wrote inadequate incident reports specifically to spark confrontations with supervisors. Apparently, orders to rewrite reports provided senior officers the opportunity to verbally express the anger and frustration they were experiencing toward the department in general.

Productivity   Firsthand observations at this department indicated that younger officers on all three shifts perceived the veterans as unproductive and lazy, perhaps largely as a result of the verbal exchanges between sergeants and veteran officers before and after each shift. Younger officers tended to maintain a social distance from veteran officers for fear that being associated with them might jeopardize their own good standing with the shift supervisor. However, after comparing shift productivity sheets between all patrol shifts for a one-month period, it became clear that there was little difference in work activity between older and younger officers. Veteran officers were issuing traffic citations, making arrests and handling service-related calls at approximately the same rate as younger officers on all shifts. What seemed to cause the perception of unproductivity for the veterans was related not to the quantity of their work, but rather to the negative attitude they often overtly displayed toward the department in front of their peers.

Recognizing expertise   The majority of veteran officers felt that the department constantly failed to recognize their expertise in such areas as firearms training, hostage negotiation and domestic conflict resolution—areas in which they could provide training for less experienced officers. More seasoned police were rarely asked to develop training classes on any of these topics, nor were they consulted by supervisors to take a leadership role in work-related situations that could utilize their expertise. Instead, less experienced officers were requested to research a subject and present their findings to the shift. This practice was perceived by veterans as a personal affront to their knowledge and experience.

Insensitivity to problems of aging   Patrol work has often been associated with younger police. The physical and emotional attributes that the job requires do cause older officers problems. In the department studied, the majority of officers over the age of 35 frequently complained of back problems and emotional stress, and felt that other "inside" assignments within the department would prolong their police career. However, special assignments out of the patrol bureau were seen as a reward for productive work and veteran officers were not perceived as productive people, nor were their typically negative attitudes perceived as benefiting the organization. Those older officers who desired a change from patrol to other parts of the department found themselves in a real dilemma. Patrol to them came to be regarded almost as a punishment for their lack of organizational conformity.

Many veterans in the study group believed that the department wanted to force them out, and most felt that their shift supervisors were out to get them. This perception was not altogether untrue, and some sergeants even expressed their frustration in attempting to force veteran officers to become more productive and respectful toward their supervisory authority. The ongoing tension between the veterans and the younger supervisors was a real source of frustration, and many supervisors verbalized a desire to see the veterans leave the department.

A final, but important, problem for long-term patrol officers lay in the physical and mental adaptations to working the graveyard shift. All 20 veterans studied claimed that, as they got older, working all night became more difficult for them but, because of the policy that made everyone rotate shifts every two years, they had to work nights. Not only did the change increase the stress level in their families, but—since it took approximately four months to adjust to this new time period—for the first four months the veterans complained of being fatigued throughout their shift. This fatigue obviously affected their productivity, which in turn reinforced the stigma of laziness that preceded them to the new shift. Thus, the new supervisors quickly validated the negative perception of the veteran's productivity passed along by other shift supervisors. This was especially true for young sergeants who threatened to discipline older officers even before they were rotated to the sergeant's shift. Many claimed that, as supervisors, they looked forward to the opportunity to straighten the "old timers" out—an attitude that likely served to heighten an already tense situation.

Conclusions

This paper has attempted to analyze those problems that older, veteran officers who work in patrol appear to experience if they remain line employees. They have been in police work for a number of years and indicate a desire to remain on the job until they are eligible for retirement.

The problems faced by veteran patrol officers pose a dilemma for both the officers themselves and the entire organization. Police managers must begin to realize that these problems will increase over time, as the number of senior police swells.

There is an obvious need for a drastically different approach in managerial techniques in order to decrease the hostility and alienation felt by older officers. Veteran officers must be brought back into the mainstream of the organization before the gap widens to the point at which these veterans become a destructive force rather than the experienced leaders they could—and should—be.

1. H. Robinette, "The Police Problem Employee," *FBI Law Enforcement Bulletin*, 1982, p. 10.
2. M. Reiser, "Some Organizational Stresses on Policemen," *Journal of Police Science and Administration*, 1974, 2:156-159.
3. J. Schwartz and C. Schwartz, "Job Stress and the Police Officer: Identifying Stress Reduction Techniques," *Stress and Police Personnel*, edited by L. Torrito and H. Vetter (Boston, MA: Allyn and Bacon, 1975) pp. 99-113.
4. P. Whisenand, *The Meaning of Police Organizations* (Englewood Cliffs, NJ: Prentice-Hall, 1978).
5. R. Clay and R. Yates, "Problem Employee Survey: An Analysis of Employee Problem Areas in Law Enforcement" (Quantico, VA: FBI Academy, 1981).
6. J. Auten, "Productivity: A Challenge for the '80s," *FBI Law Enforcement Bulletin*, 1982, p. 5.
7. M. Pogrebin, "Service and Law Enforcement Functions: An Ideological Conflict for Police," *The Police Chief*, 1980, 47:48-50
8. W. Carey, *Documenting Employee Discipline and Dismissal* (Salem, MA: Options Press, 1985).
9. J. Preiss and Erlich, *An Examination of Role Theory: The Case of State Police* (Lincoln, NE: University of Nebraska Press, 1966).
10. T. Eisenberg, "Labor Management Relations and Psychological Stress: View from the Bottom," *The Police Chief*, 1975, 42:54-58.
11. H. Levinson, "On Being a Middle-Aged Manager," *Harvard Business Review*, 1969, 47:55-67.
12. M. Harmon, "Social Equity in Public Administration," *Public Administration Review*, 1974, 34:29-34.

Employee Drug Testing in Police Departments

Edward F. Connors III, Hugh Nugent,
J. Thomas McEwen, and Barbara Manili

The availability and widespread use of illegal drugs is a cause of national alarm today. Reports of drug abuse come from every segment of our society. Thus it should come as no surprise that the police have not been immune to the contagion of drug abuse. Police officers experience stress and trauma in their jobs, and some may turn to drugs as a form of coping.

Drug use by police officers is now an important issue for every police chief in the nation. The problem is receiving national attention because of its potential threat to the integrity of law enforcement and the safety of the community.

To learn how police departments are addressing this problem, the National Institute of Justice sponsored a telephone survey of 33 major police departments. The research was conducted by the Institute for Law and Justice, Inc., of Alexandria, Virginia. Of the 33 departments surveyed, 24 had drug testing programs. These departments explained their testing procedures, selection process, and what procedures were used after a positive test. They also discussed whether treatment programs were available, and whether random testing had ever been considered. Departments provided information on the types of tests conducted, the administration of the tests, the procedures used to establish chain of custody, and the costs of the tests.

Key findings from the survey indicated that:

An earlier version of this article was published in October 1986 as part of the *Research in Brief* series of the U.S. Department of Justice, National Institute of Justice. Points of view or opinions expressed in this publication are those of the authors and do not necessarily represent the official position or policies of the U.S. Department of Justice.

1. Seventy-three percent of the departments surveyed were conducting drug screening tests of applicants.
2. Virtually all departments had written policies and procedures for conducting tests when there was reason to suspect that officers were using illegal drugs.
3. Twenty-one percent said they were considering mandatory testing of all officers.
4. Twenty-four percent indicated that treatment (rather than dismissal) would be appropriate for officers under some circumstances, generally depending on the type of drug and severity of the problem.

These results show that many police managers are taking steps to make their departments as drug-free as possible.

Further impetus for action has come from the International Association of Chiefs of Police (IACP), which developed a model drug testing policy for local police departments to consider in identifying and dealing with the use of illegal drugs by police officers. The policy calls for:

1. Testing applicants and recruits for drug or narcotics use as part of their pre-employment medical exams
2. Testing a current employee when documentation indicates that the employee is impaired or incapable of performing assigned duties, or experiences reduced productivity, excessive vehicle accidents, high absenteeism, or other behavior inconsistent with previous performance
3. Requiring current sworn employees assigned to drug, narcotics, or vice enforcement units to undergo periodic drug tests.

Many police departments already have policies along these lines. The IACP's endorsement of these steps may encourage other departments to take similar action to deal with employee drug abuse.

This article reviews both the approaches of private industry to the problem and the use of drug testing in police departments. It summarizes the technology of drug tests, the alternatives used by police administrators for dealing with officers found to use drugs, and legal and union issues surrounding drug tests. It also presents other survey results to show the trend in current practices.

Employee drug testing in private industry

Approximately one-fourth of the country's Fortune 500 firms now test job applicants for drugs, up from 10 percent three years ago. In addition to firms in the aerospace, airline, and railroad industries, major firms with applicant drug screening programs include IBM, DuPont, AT&T, General Motors, Ford Motor Company, Exxon, Mobil, Boise Cascade, the *New York Times*, and Capital Cities/ABC.

Advocates of job applicant testing say that the benefits include higher quality applicants and, after hiring, reduced absenteeism, higher productivity, and fewer accidents. Some private employers maintain that increased applicant drug testing will become a significant economic deterrent to drug abuse in society, as more and more people face a choice between using drugs or finding a job. On the other hand, a few firms, including Hewlett-Packard and McDonnell Douglas, have publicly opposed urinalysis testing of employees as an invasion of privacy and do not test applicants or current employees.

Some firms require urinalysis tests for current employees under certain conditions. Typically, tests may be conducted when there is reasonable suspicion of drug abuse because of job performance problems, accidents, or for safety or security reasons such as test-flying aircraft and handling classified materials. In addition to urinalysis, private employers have taken other measures to curb drug use, possession, and sale in the workplace. These include the use of local undercover police, drug-sniffing dogs, private investigative and security firms, and searches of employees' lockers and desks.

Because drug addiction and alcoholism are protected handicaps under the Federal Rehabilitation Act of 1973, employees who work for firms with federal government contracts may be legally entitled to seek rehabilitation before being terminated. Employers may also have a legal duty under state or local statutes to "reasonably accommodate" employees with drug abuse problems. But the duty and desire to offer treatment opportunities must often be balanced with the responsibility to provide all employees with a safe workplace and maintain the quality of products and services.

About 30 percent of the Fortune 500 largest industrial corporations have in-house employee assistance programs. Other private employers make referrals and maintain policies that encourage employees to seek treatment. In some companies paid sick leave policies enable employees to enter treatment without loss of salary. Xerox has a toll-free hotline for employees who are reluctant to approach immediate supervisors about substance abuse problems.

Private employers, in the absence of local ordinances or union agreements, appear to have a greater degree of freedom than government agencies in developing drug abuse policies. However, the courts have not resolved many of the relevant legal issues, and a number of lawsuits are pending that challenge both the reliability and constitutionality of private sector drug screening tests and policies. Issues include the company's right to information about an employee's private life, the use of relatively expensive corroborative tests for both applicants and current employees whose initial test results are positive, prosecutors' access to company testing records, the submission of policies for collective bargaining with labor unions, the employer's obligation to inform employees that urine samples in routine physicals will be analyzed for drugs, and other privacy and confidentiality issues.

Participants at the March 1986 National Institute of Drug Abuse conference on drug testing in the workplace reached consensus on a number of recommendations for private employers: inform all employees who will be tested, do not test without clear evidence of job performance problems, corroborate all positive tests, protect the confidentiality of the results, and accompany urinalysis testing with opportunities for rehabilitation. Many of these measures may be applicable to police departments.

Testing police applicants and employees

Drug tests have become a key feature of many police department programs to detect and deter the use of illicit substances by employees. Testing may occur as part of the screening process for applicants, as a requirement during the probationary period, as a condition of accepting a transfer, promotion, or assignment to a sensitive position, when officers are suspected of drug use because of behavior or work performance, or as part of a required annual physical.

Testing applicants Table 1 shows the policies of the local police departments in the survey that had some type of drug testing program. Of the 24 departments, 15 conducted tests of job applicants, and in all 15 departments applicants were rejected when the tests were positive. The survey did not request information on the percentage of applicants rejected. However, local newspapers have reported that 20 to 25 percent of the applicants for uniformed positions in some large urban departments have shown positive urinalysis results.

Table 1. Job categories and events tested in surveyed departments (N = 24).

Job category and event tested	Number of departments	Percent
Job applicants	15	62.5
Probationary officers	5	20.8
Officers seeking transfers to sensitive jobs	3	12.5
Officers in sensitive jobs	4	16.7
Officers suspected of drug use	18	75.0
After auto accidents	2	8.3
Scheduled testing	1	4.2

In Texas, state law places emphasis on law enforcement's responsibility to hire drug-free employees. Specifically, the law states that a person may not become a peace officer, jailer or guard of a county jail, or a reserve law enforcement officer unless the person is "examined by a licensed physician and is declared in writing by the physician to show no trace of drug dependency or illegal drug usage after a physical examination, blood test, or other medical test." In disputed cases, an applicant may be ordered to submit to an examination by a state-appointed physician for certification that the applicant is not dependent on drugs and does not use illegal drugs.

Testing probationary officers   Testing probationary officers is a standard procedure in some police departments. The New York City Police Department recently administered urinalysis tests for drugs, including marijuana, to more than 5,000 probationary officers. Only 18 officers (0.36 percent) showed positive results. While the probationary officers knew they would be tested three times between their recruitment date and the end of their 18-month probationary period, they did not know the exact dates of testing.

Testing officers in sensitive jobs   Some departments require testing as a condition for transfers or promotions to sensitive jobs such as vice and narcotics, internal affairs, SWAT teams, and data processing. Officers may be asked to sign an agreement that, as part of accepting a new position, they will take periodic drug tests to demonstrate freedom from drug dependency and abuse. In these instances, the testing is considered voluntary and is a condition of seeking and accepting a new position.

Testing tenured officers   Departments test tenured officers for several reasons. In many instances officers can be required to submit to a test when they are suspected of drug use. Suspicion can occur as a result of a job performance review, a specific incident (such as a traffic accident or shooting), or an internal affairs investigation.

Periodic testing of tenured officers may also be a precondition for employment. For example, Boston transit police officers agree to allow periodic testing when they are hired, and one department in the survey incudes a drug test as part of an officer's annual physical.

Scheduled versus random testing   One of the most controversial issues involves random testing of officers. Union opposition to random testing of tenured officers is almost universal and, as noted in the discussion of legal issues that concludes this chapter, the Supreme Court has not yet ruled on whether random tests violate the Fourth Amendment rights of employees.

Scheduled testing, such as testing as part of the annual physical exam for all employees, has not been as severely criticized as random testing. Scheduled testing allows an employee to stop using drugs temporarily just prior to the tests, but it still may deter some officers from using drugs. It has the additional advantage of becoming an expected, routine part of the physical examination, which reduces objections based on privacy issues.

Technology of drug testing

A number of questions and issues have been raised about the types and accuracy of tests departments use to detect drugs. Most departments surveyed administer an initial test, such as EMIT (Enzyme Multiplied Immunoassay Technique), followed by confirmatory tests for samples with positive results, using gas chromatography/mass spectrometry. Of the 18 departments responding to a question about who conducts the tests, 12 said they use outside private labs; 3 use their jurisdictions' crime labs; 1 uses its state health department; 1 uses a local hospital; and 1 uses the health unit of the police department.

The EMIT test is popular because it is relatively inexpensive and has a reputation for accuracy. Gas chromatography and gas chromatography/mass spectrometry are even more accurate and are considered necessary to ensure that the initial EMIT results are correct. Even when both tests are used, a possibility remains that "false positives" will occur. For this reason, most departments conduct a further investigation for employees who show positive results on these tests and contest the results.

Police departments must also consider other aspects of drug screening technology. For example, "threshold" levels must be established to determine when a result should be considered positive. This is analogous to the standard 0.10 percent for blood-alcohol content to presume intoxication. However, drug urinalysis tests are used to prove an individual has recently used drugs, while blood-alcohol tests are used to determine impairment at the time of arrest.

If the threshold level is too low, then the test results may be considered positive even though the individual may have been exposed to the drug in a passive setting such as breathing marijuana smoke in a closed room. At the other extreme, if the threshold level is set too high, the dependent user may not provide a positive result from the test.

Procedural safeguards also must be established when conducting these tests. Tests should be administered as though the results will become part of a legal proceeding. The chain of custody must be documented—records must be kept on everyone who physically handles the sample—and all samples must be properly labeled, stored, and protected in an appropriate manner. Further, personnel who supervise and administer the testing process must be properly trained, and laboratory technicians must be experienced and certified in the use of the test equipment.

Counseling versus termination

Police administrators face difficult decisions when an officer tests positive, and further investigation confirms that the officer is a drug user. Even though the officer's job performance may be exemplary, many police chiefs agree that termination is the only solution, at least in part to protect the department from civil liability for knowingly employing drug abusers.

The decision to terminate an officer is generally based on several considerations. First, the officer has possessed an illegal substance and therefore has committed a crime. Second, the officer has associated with known felons in the acquisition of the illegal drug and therefore may compromise the integrity of the department.

On the other hand, some police administrators have endorsed programs similar to the Boston Police Stress Program. Assistance programs are available for officers who have problems with alcohol, drugs, or a combination of these substances. In some agencies, however, participation in programs not endorsed by the department does not protect the employee from disciplinary action if the department discovers the employee's drug problems. As a result, employees who voluntarily enter assistance programs often feel additional pressure to make sure their participation is not known to members of the department.

A number of departments are taking steps to make recruits and officers more aware of the problems associated with drug abuse. The New York Police Department has developed a drug awareness videotape and a three-hour drug awareness workshop. In addition, the training manuals of the New York Police Academy now include a special booklet on drug abuse. In Philadelphia, the Fraternal Order of Police has produced a videotape encouraging officers with drug use problems to seek professional help. Police managers may use these training sessions to clarify departmental policy and to ensure that officers have accurate expectations with regard to privacy issues and sanctions surrounding drug abuse.

Legal standards for testing employees for drugs

In 1989, the United States Supreme Court decided three drug-testing cases, clarifying but not completely resolving some of the legal issues implicit in testing.

In two cases, over strong dissents, the Court upheld the constitutionality of testing employees against Fourth Amendment challenges. Both cases were brought by employee unions challenging testing of their members. Significantly, neither case involved a specific action that had been taken against an employee who had already been disciplined, fired, or prosecuted because of a test.

In *Skinner* v. *Railway Labor Executives' Association,*[1] the Court reviewed the regulations of the Federal Railroad Administration (FRA) mandating blood and urine testing of employees involved in certain kinds of train accidents. The FRA regulations also authorized, but did not require, railroads to administer breath and urine tests to employees who violate certain safety rules. In soliciting public comment prior to adoption of the regulation, FRA had stated that between 1972 and 1983, there had been at least 21 significant railroad accidents involving drug or alcohol use, with 25 fatalities, 61 non-fatal injuries, and property damage at $19 million. There were 17 fatalities to operating employees working on rolling stock that involved drugs or alcohol.[2]

The regulations required "post-accident toxicological testing" after "major train accidents," "impact accidents," and any train incident involving a fatality of an on-duty railroad employee.[3] The regulations also authorized testing "for cause" after accidents where supervisors had reasonable suspicion that an employee's acts or omissions had contributed to the occurrence or severity of an accident. Testing "for cause" was also authorized in the event of certain specific rule violations, and where supervisors had reasonable suspicion that an employee was under the influence of alcohol or drugs.[4]

At the beginning of its analysis, the Court held that, even though the tests are conducted by private employers, they are subject to the Fourth Amendment because United States government requires the employers to administer the tests.[5] Thus, the principles of *Skinner* are applicable to the public employees with whom we are concerned in this article.

The Court also held that the drug tests required by FRA—including blood, urine, and breath tests—constituted searches within the meaning of the Fourth Amendment,[6] bringing the justices to the question of whether they were constitutionally reasonable.

The Court has recognized "special needs" that make the probable cause and search warrant requirements impracticable. In doing so, the Court has attempted to determine whether governmental interests outweigh individuals' privacy interests in particular contexts, and to rule accordingly.[7] In *Skinner*, the Court found that the government's interest in regulating conduct of railroad employees to ensure safety is a special need.

Individual privacy interests ordinarily are protected by the warrant requirement and process, which assure the citizen that the intrusion into privacy is authorized by law, narrowly limited in scope, and not random or arbitrary. But in the circumstances covered by the regulation, the standardized tests and the minimal discretion involved in their administration left virtually nothing for a neutral magistrate to evaluate. The Court therefore concluded that drug tests under the FRA rules did not require warrants.[8]

Still, the general rule has required probable cause, even when searches are permitted without warrants. Where a balancing of government and privacy interests precludes a showing of probable cause, the Court has still insisted on "some quantum of individualized suspicion." But, in *Skinner*, the Court held:

In limited circumstances, where the privacy interests implicated by the search are minimal, and where an important governmental interest furthered by the intrusion would be placed in jeopardy by a requirement of individualized suspicion, a search may be reasonable despite the absence of such suspicion. We believe this is true of the intrusions in question here.[9]

The Court noted that FRA breath tests involved no invasion of the body and that urine testing was being done with a sensitivity to personal privacy. Since employees of any enterprise are rarely free to come and go as they please, the Court reasoned, these intrusions authorized by the FRA regulations are limited, involve only minimal inconvenience, and, therefore, are constitutionally reasonable.[10]

According to the Court, the privacy interests of affected employees are diminished because of their participation in an industry already heavily regulated to ensure safety, "a goal dependent, in large part, on the health and fitness of covered employees."[11] Further:

By contrast, the government interest in testing without a showing of individualized suspicion is compelling. Employees subject to the tests discharge duties fraught with such risks of injury to others that even a momentary lapse of attention can have disastrous consequences.[12]

The Court went on to state that the FRA regulations provide an effective deterrent against use of drugs or alcohol by employees. In the Court's view, the testing procedures and post-accident testing would also provide valuable data on causes of major accidents and desirable remedial steps. Both these benefits would be lost, according to the Court, if particularized suspicion were required.[13] Although Justice Stevens concurred in the majority opinion, he did not agree with these conclusions regarding deterrence. In Justice Stevens' view, workers who are not deterred from drug or alcohol abuse by the danger of serious injury to themselves are also unlikely to be deterred by the additional threat of loss of employment.[14]

Justice Marshall, joined by Justice Brennan, dissented, stating that the Court had "taken its longest step yet toward reading the probable cause requirement out of the Fourth Amendment."[15] Criticizing several recent Court rulings that allowed "special needs" to displace warrant and probable cause requirements, Justice Marshall said that "the process by which a constitutional 'requirement' can be dispensed with as 'impracticable' is an elusive one to me."[16]

In *National Treasury Employees Union* v. *Von Raab*,[17] the Supreme Court examined United States Customs Service regulations requiring urinalysis tests of employees seeking transfer to three different types of positions: (1) those with direct involvement in drug interdiction or enforcement of related laws; (2) those requiring carrying of firearms; (3) those requiring handling of classified information (that might fall into the hands of drug dealers if employees became subject to blackmail as a result of their own drug abuse).[18] Under the regulations, urine specimens were to be tested for presence of marijuana, cocaine, opiates, amphetamines, and phencyclidine. Customs employees who tested positive for drugs were subject to dismissal but, unless employees consented in writing, test results could not be turned over to any other agency, including criminal prosecutors.[19] Justice Kennedy wrote for the majority, and followed the line of reasoning he had set out in his opinion for the *Skinner* majority. Acknowledging that the tests were searches as defined by the Fourth Amendment, Justice Kennedy wrote that "our decision in *Railway Labor Executives* reaffirms the longstanding principle that neither a warrant nor probable cause, nor, indeed, any measure of individualized suspicion, is an indispensable component of reasonableness in every circumstance."[20] The Customs Service's program was not designed for the ordinary purposes of law enforcement, and its test results could not be used in criminal prosecutions. In these circumstances, the majority agreed, individual privacy expectations had to be weighed against the government's interest in deterring drug use among aspirants to sensitive Customs positions.[21]

In such circumstances, the majority concluded, warrants would add little or nothing to personal privacy. Customs employees knew the testing procedures and requirements for these positions, and the uniformity of the procedures and requirements meant that independent magistrates had nothing to review.[22] In addition, the majority stated, employees involved in interdiction or enforcement, or who carry firearms should expect reasonable inquiries into their fitness and probity.[23]

The union had argued that the program was unjustified because it was not based on any real belief that drug testing would reveal employees' drug abuse, and that such an unproductive scheme could not justify intrusion on so many employees' Fourth Amendment interests.[24] Convinced by the government's arguments that the interest in safeguarding national borders outweighed the privacy interests in question, the Court rejected these arguments as they applied to employees involved in interdiction and enforcement and to those who carried firearms.[25]

However, the Court did not find the same justification for application of the rule to employees with access to classified information. The Customs Service had listed the following positions as covered by the requirement: accountant, accounting technician, animal caretaker, attorney, baggage clerk, co-op student, electric equipment repairer, mail clerk/assistant, and messenger. The Court questioned whether the Customs Service's inclusion of these categories into the affected classes was too broad, and sent the case back for further consideration of this issue.[26]

Justice Marshall, again joined by Justice Brennan, dissented for the same reasons he articulated in *Skinner.*[27] Justice Scalia, joined by Justice Stevens, also dissented, stating that he had joined the railroad case's majority opinion because of the demonstrated frequency of drug and alcohol abuse by the targeted class of employees. But he declined to join the Customs decision "because neither frequency of use nor connection to harm is demonstrated or even likely. In my view the Customs Service rules are a kind of immolation of privacy and human dignity in symbolic opposition to drug use."[28] Bitingly, Justice Scalia wrote:

What is absent in the Government's justifications—notably absent, revealingly absent, and as far as I am concerned, dispositively absent—is the recitation of *even a single instance* in which any of the speculated horribles actually occurred: an instance, that is, in which the cause of bribe-taking, or of poor aim, or of unsympathetic law enforcement, or of compromise of classified information, was drug use [emphasis in original].[29]

On June 19, 1989, the Supreme Court decided a third case involving drug testing, *Consolidated Rail Corporation* v. *Railway Labor Executives' Association.*[30] Conrail had unilaterally added urinalysis drug screening to the periodic and return-from-leave physical examinations it had required for several years. The case turns on whether this change gave rise to a "major" or a "minor" dispute under the Railway Labor Act, but adds little to discussion of the constitutionality of drug testing programs.

There are three important points to be made about these cases. First, in none of them does the Supreme Court address questions concerning the reasonableness of *random* drug testing programs.

Second, where there is substantial history of alcohol or drug problem in the industry, or where there is reasonable suspicion about individual employees, a majority of the Supreme Court found drug testing reasonable within the Fourth Amendment. But such testing was tied to specific occurrences, such as serious accidents or rules violations. This is the thrust of *Skinner* v. *Railway Labor Executives' Association.*[31]

Third, only a narrow majority of the Court is willing to sanction drug testing that applies to specific personnel positions, rather than to specific individuals or specific occurrences. Further, in such cases, the Court also must be persuaded that the nature of the position in question justifies the intrusion on individual privacy. When it addressed these questions in *National Treasury Employees Union v. Von Raab*,[32] the Court sent the case back for further consideration of the reasonableness of testing employees who are required to handle classified material. The majority said:

Upon remand the court of appeals should examine the criteria used by the Service in determining what materials are classified and in deciding whom to test under this rubric. In assessing the reasonableness of requiring tests of these employees, the court should also consider pertinent information bearing upon the employees' privacy expectations, as well as the supervision to which these employees are already subject.[33]

Thus, the Supreme Court's decisions do not sanction sweeping drug testing without substantial justification—in the history of an industry, in reasonable suspicion raised by an individual's behavior, in the risks entailed in a particular kind of employment—to give the public interest greater weight than the intrusion on individual privacy.

1. 109 S. Ct. 1402 (1989).
2. *Ibid.* at 1407-1408.
3. *Ibid.* at 1408-1409.
4. *Ibid.* at 1409-1410.
5. *Ibid.* at 1411-1412.
6. *Ibid.* at 1412-1413.
7. *Ibid.* at 1414.
8. *Ibid.* at 1415-1416.
9. *Ibid.* at 1417.
10. *Ibid.* at 1417-1418.
11. *Ibid.* at 1418.
12. *Ibid.* at 1419.
13. *Ibid.* at 1419-1420.
14. *Ibid.* at 1422.
15. *Ibid.* at 1423.
16. *Ibid.*
17. 109 S.Ct. 1384 (1989).
18. *Ibid.* at 1388.
19. *Ibid.* at 1389.
20. *Ibid.* at 1390.
21. *Ibid.* at 1390-91.
22. *Ibid.* at 1391.
23. *Ibid.* at 1394.
24. *Ibid.* at 1394-95.
25. *Ibid.* at 1396.
26. *Ibid.* at 1397.
27. *Ibid.* at 1398.
28. *Ibid.*
29. *Ibid.* at 1399-1400.
30. 57 Law Week 4742.
31. 109 S. Ct. 1402 (1989).
32. *Ibid.* at 1384.
33. *Ibid.* at 1397.

Additional Recommended Readings

Carter, David, and Darrel Stephens. *Drug Abuse by Police Officers: An Analysis of Critical Policy Issues.* Springfield, IL: Charles C Thomas, 1988. A useful guide to recognizing and dealing with the problem of substance abuse among police personnel.

Carter, David, Allen Sapp, and Darrel Stephens. *The State of Police Education: Policy Directions for the 21st Century.* Washington, DC: Police Executive Research Forum, 1988. Includes the results of a survey of police educational attainment and suggests that emphasis on higher education for police did not end with cutbacks in federal funds for this purpose. Especially useful in formulation of policies related to officers' education.

Eck, John E. *Using Research: A Primer for Law Enforcement Managers.* Washington, DC: Police Executive Research Forum, 1984. Eck, an operations researcher, bridges the gap between academic researchers and police practitioners. Here, he tells what he knows about this art and takes the mystery out of researchers' graphs, charts, and statistics. His purpose is not to make researchers out of police officials but to turn police officials into intelligent consumers of research.

Fogelson, Robert M. *Big-City Police.* Cambridge, MA: Harvard University Press, 1977. The definitive history of the development of urban policing in the United States. Fogelson traces the police and their scandals and reforms from the early nineteenth century to the mid-1970s. In the process, he provides us with a prognosis for the future.

Goldstein, Herman. "Improving Policing: A Problem-Oriented Approach." 25 *Crime and Delinquency* 236 (April 1979). This is the seminal article in which Goldstein first defined problem-oriented policing. One of the most influential essays of the past several decades, it should be read by anyone who bears responsibility for police policy or operations.

Higdon, Richard K., and Philip G. Huber. *How to Fight Fear: The COPE Program Package.* Washington, DC: Police Executive Research Forum, 1987. Two veteran police officers describe the organization, management, training, and procedures used in Baltimore County, Maryland's successful Citizen Oriented Police Enforcement (COPE) program. Built upon Goldstein's work, COPE has substantially reduced crime and calls for service.

Matulia, Kenneth R. *A Balance of Forces.* 2d ed. Gaithersburg, MD: International Association of Chiefs of Police, 1985. This study contains the most comprehensive data on justifiable homicides by American police officers. The data are not well presented or analyzed but are informative, and the report offers excellent model deadly force and firearms policies, with commentary.

Muir, William K. *Police: Streetcorner Politicians.* Chicago: University of Chicago Press, 1977. An intensive study of 28 police patrol officers that attempts to define police professionalism and concludes that it consists of an understanding of human suffering and the ability to apply coercive police power in a moral way. Muir, a political scientist, then suggests means of developing these traits in police officers.

Murphy, Gerald R. *Special Care: Improving the Police Response to the Mentally Ill.* Washington, DC: Police Executive Research Forum, 1986. As the population of American institutions for the retarded and the mentally ill has decreased, police encounters with the mentally disabled have increased and sometimes ended in tragedy. This study surveys relevant literature, describes exemplary programs for police interaction with the mentally disabled and for cooperation with mental health professionals, and makes many specific recommendations for training and policy.

Reuss-Ianni, Elizabeth. *Two Cultures of Policing: Street Cops and Management Cops.* New Brunswick, NJ: Transaction Books, 1983. As those inside policing have long known, police agencies include two cultures: that of the "street cop" and that of the "management cop." Reuss-Ianni's exhaustive study of street-level policing leads her to identify a "cop's code" of behavior and to conclude that the conflict between the two cultures of policing is the major organizational dilemma of contemporary police. This is excellent scholarship and not merely an ivory-tower exercise.

Sherman, Lawrence W., and Richard A. Berk. "The Specific Deterrent Effect of Arrests for Domestic Assault." *American Sociological Review* 49 (1984): 261–272. This report of the controversial Minneapolis Domestic Violence Experiment suggests that arrest, rather than mediation, is the most effective means of preventing future assaultive behavior in the home. Marred by some unavoidable methodological problems, the experiment is currently undergoing replication in several jurisdictions.

Skolnick, Jerome H., and David H. Bayley. *The New Blue Line.* New York: Free Press, 1986. Two leading police scholars look at managerial variation and innovation (along with some stagnation) in six major cities. This important book contains sociological in-

sights as well as tips useful to police and government administrators.

*Standards for Law Enforcement
Agencies.* Fairfax, VA: Commission on Accreditation for Law Enforcement Agencies, Inc., 1987.
Defines the state of the art of police policy and practice and is extremely useful whether or not
application for accreditation is
intended.

Wilson, James Q., and George L.
Kelling. "Broken Windows." *The
Atlantic Monthly* 29 (March 1982).
Wilson and Kelling argue for a return to foot patrol and the notion
of police officer as defender of the
community, its stability, and its
values. Their controversial work
questions the narrow crime-
fighting orientation of recent definitions of professionalism. An
articulate and well-reasoned critique of their ideas and arguments is Samuel Walker's "Broken Windows and Fractured
History: The Use and Misuse of
History in Recent Police Patrol
Analysis." *Justice Quarterly* 1
(1984).

Practical Management Series

**Police Practice in the '90s:
Key Management Issues**

Text type
Century Expanded

Composition
Applied Graphics Technologies
Washington, D.C.

Printing and binding
R.R. Donnelley & Sons Company
Harrisonburg, Virginia

Cover design
Rebecca Geanaros